THE WORLD'S BEST
Starters

THE WORLD'S BEST

Starters

ANTIPASTI • HORS D'OEUVRES • TAPAS • ZAKUSKI
APERITIVOS • VORSPEISEN • ANTOJITOS • MEZEDES

Roger Hicks and Frances Schultz

ROSENDALE PRESS

Copyright © Roger Hicks and Frances Schultz

First Published in Great Britain in 1994 by
Rosendale Press
Premier House
10 Greycoat Place
London SW1P 1SB

Photographs by Roger Hicks and Frances Schultz
Photo page 97 by Robin Chanda
Book designed by Robert Updegraff
Production: Edward Allhusen, Old House Books

ISBN 1 872803 11 3

Printed and bound in Italy by
G. Canale & Co. SpA, Turin

British Library Cataloguing in Publication Data
A catalogue record for theis book is available from the British Library

Frontispiece: *Greek vegetables with eggs, an ideal vegetarian supper.*

CONTENTS

Zakuski, little Russian bites of smoked fish.

INTRODUCTION

MAKING A MEAL OF STARTERS

In almost every language except English there is a term for "little foods", things which are neither merely appetizers nor formal meals. Typically, they originated as appetizers, and they can still be served that way; but they can also replace the meal they were supposed to precede.

This is a style of eating which is becoming increasingly fashionable. You can eat as much or as little as you want: you can eat whenever you want, from mid-morning to midnight and beyond; and increasingly, you can eat whatever you want, from the cuisines of the world. In these pages you will find some recipes which are so quick and easy that they become stand-bys: food for whenever you are in a hurry or haven't time to buy anything elaborate, let alone prepare it. There are others which are perfectly suited to a sort of rolling party, where friends drop by and you prepare some of this, and some of that, and co-opt your friends to help you make a little of something else. And, of course, many of them can be served as a formal beginning to a grand meal.

There are also many dishes which you may have encountered when you were travelling, or perhaps merely read about, and thought, "I wonder what that is?". This is how we acquired most of the recipes here: we tried them, or read about them, or heard friends raving about them, and we set out to find out how they were made. Sometimes we just asked; sometimes we consulted cookery books, in half a dozen different languages; and sometimes we had to experiment, comparing what we had tried with several different recipes until we came closest to recreating the original taste.

Inevitably, there are omissions. This is partly because of limitations of space, and partly because there are many dishes where the ingredients are difficult or even impossible for many people to find: for example, the various Spanish dishes involving tiny elvers require access to a source of baby eels. Another reason for omissions is pure personal taste: neither of us particularly likes whitebait, so we felt we could not give a recipe which we could not fairly stand by. Also, we omitted a number of recipes which are delicious but time-consuming, on the grounds that there are plenty of easy, delicious appetizers which require far less effort and which fit in better with a busy lifestyle. After all, appetizers are supposed to be quick: they were originally what you gave people while they were waiting for the main course. We have, however, included other recipes which do take a certain amount of time, but are worth it.

Although we have striven for the utmost possible authenticity, there are also suggestions on how to vary the authentic recipes. For example, sesame oil is very rarely used in European food preparation, but as a substitute for olive oil in, for instance, bean salad, it is superb. Please, please vary the recipes to suit your own taste. Countless times, we have encountered cookery books which say that French cooks always do this, or Mexican cooks always do that, or Indian cooks always do something else, when we know from personal observation that the writer is wrong. Our recipes will work the first time you try them, but if you like your food spicier or less spicy, or with more or less oil or garlic, or more cooked or less cooked, then feel free to adjust the recipe accordingly. In particular, if you are using the American system of measuring (by cups instead of weight), remember that this is a very imprecise method of measurement, especially when you are dealing with chopped vegetables, for example, where weight is a far more reliable guide.

Also, serve everything at the temperature which suits you best. Some dishes do have to be served piping hot, and a few have to be served chilled: but often, the distinction between "hot" and "room temperature" is negotiable. For example, *nachos* should be brought to the table hot and freshly assembled; but you can then pick at them as they cool, and even after an hour or so they can still be delicious – though eventually, anything can lose its charms. The exact life of a dish will depend on the ingredients, the cook, the conditions in which it is kept, and the fussiness of whoever is eating it, but there are comparatively few appetizers which can survive overnight. Where long preparation in advance is feasible, we have said so. We have also indicated where these little foods *should* be served chilled; where they *can* be served chilled; and where they are much better if they are allowed to come to room temperature before they are served.

Another point concerning the life of a dish (assuming your hungry guests do not fall upon it immediately) is that the fresher it is, the better it is likely to look: old appetizers often look (as well as taste) wilted and soft. Anything that appears in this book, though, you should be able to duplicate, because we have used the very minimum of "tricks" for the photography. We feel quite strongly about this, because a lot of food shots are faked to the point of inedibility. We have only used three "tricks". One is that the food is slightly undercooked (which looks more natural in a photograph). The second is that we have occasionally used oil to create an extra gloss because otherwise food dries out under the lights. The third is that we have sometimes over-thickened sauces. A sauce which looks great for a few minutes, and which is normally added just before serving, can start to spread or to lose oil at the edges if it is left to sit for even five or ten minutes. You wouldn't notice it on a domestic buffet, but you would in a photograph.

There are quite a lot of short cuts in these pages but surprisingly, they are "authentic" in the sense that this is how things are made today. For instance, almost no-one makes their own *escabeche* of tuna or sardine any more, and no-one fillets and salts anchovies at home. Even the best *tapas* bars or domestic

Italian cooks use cans for some things – so you will find canned ingredients in this book. If you are eating them on their own, the difference between the home-made variety and the canned variety is clear, but you don't eat them on their own: you mix them with things, spice them, flavour them, and end up with something where you probably couldn't tell whether you were eating home-made or canned.

Nowhere have we advocated the purchase of ready-made food that is clearly inferior to what you make yourself (such as sugary, starch-thickened dips), but there are plenty of places where the commercial product is perfectly acceptable, such as pickled fish. If it's feasible or desirable to make your own, we tell you how: but most people don't smoke their own salmon, for instance, so there are some places where we assume you will be using commercially prepared ingredients.

By and large, the recipes here are for surprisingly healthy food using natural ingredients with the minimum of preparation. But some of them are inclined to be rather high in calories, often because they are fried or because a good deal of butter or oil is used in their preparation. One thing you will not find in these pages is much "political correctness". Where an original recipe calls for cholesterol-laden ingredients, we specify them. If you want to use substitutes such as low-fat mayonnaise, on your own head be it.

The book is arranged, very roughly, in order of time and effort required: it begins with caviar, which requires only that you be skilful with a can opener, and then progresses through food which requires more and more preparation. The recipes came from many sources in many countries, but this does not mean that you cannot mix and match to your heart's content. The Spanish and Italians are well presented here (by *tapas* and *antipasti*), but you will also find Russians (*zakuski*), Mexicans (*antojitos*), Greeks (*mezedes*), French (of course *hors d'oeuvres*) and a Central European school represented by German *vorspeisen* – to say nothing of the individual dishes such as Japanese *sashimi* and *sushi*, Indian *pakoras* and *samosas*, Central American *chiles rellenos* and more. The only thing to add is *bon appetit* – however that translates in your language.

All recipes serve 4 unless indicated otherwise.

SOMETHING
FROM NOTHING

One of the great attractions of eating the kind of food in this book is that you can make a lot from nothing – or to be more precise, that you can make up a series of attractive and appetizing dishes from food that you have in your store cupboard, your larder, your refrigerator, your freezer and (with any luck) your garden. This is enormously useful when friends come by at short notice; when you get home too late to shop but don't want to eat out; or when you just plain forget, or don't feel like going to the shops.

GARNISHES

Much of the secret of successful appetizers is in the garnishes, which add both visual appeal and (in most cases) counterpoint of flavour and texture. The plainest dishes, which no-one would look twice at without their garnishes, can become feasts with the proper garnishes – see page 38 for bean salads, for example.

THE STORE CUPBOARD

The store cupboard is for cans, jars and packets with a long shelf life. Some of the "store cupboard" items here should be stored in the refrigerator once they have been opened.

Anchovies: The pungency of anchovies adds a kick to all kinds of things when they are used as a garnish, and they can also be chopped or pounded and used as a flavouring agent. Two or three small cans of anchovies are an essential in the store cupboard.

Beans Canned beans of various kinds form the basis of several appetizers, as already mentioned. If you have the time, you can also soak and cook dried beans; the texture is often superior to that of waterlogged canned beans. At the very least, keep butter beans and chickpeas (garbanzo beans).

Capers Even if you do not like whole capers, they are an essential ingredient in some sauces, and a good foil to bland or fatty flavours; and they do make a pretty garnish.

Caviar Sturgeon caviar, the real thing, is delicious but expensive and demands some care in conservation; but the eggs of lesser fish make an excellent garnish, as described on pages 14 and 116.

Cornichons Like capers, the taste of these small, salty gherkins is a bit too much for some people. Even those who like them are accustomed to using them in moderation. Again, like capers, they are a valuable foil to some flavours, and they make a pretty garnish.

Exotic Vegetables Canned or bottled palm hearts, artichoke hearts and asparagus last for a very long time and are ideal for entertaining unexpected company or for cheering yourself up on a dull day.

Flour As well as ordinary wheat flour, gram flour (*besan*) is used in Indian cookery to make batter for *pakoras* (page 96). These are surprisingly quick to make, especially if you have a deep-fryer.

Herbs Ideally, keep wild herbs growing in your garden or in a herb-pot. Otherwise, or in addition, keep the following dried herbs: basil, mint, dill, oregano, parsley, rosemary, sage and thyme.

Mushrooms Canned mushrooms are grossly inferior to fresh, but in an emergency – for example to make *spiedini* – they are a lot better than nothing.

Mustard Powdered or pre-mixed hot English mustard improves many sauces and emulsifies vinaigrettes. The milder French and other mustards are mainly served as accompaniments.

Oil There are endless oils available, but the three that we use most are extra virgin olive oil, sesame oil and walnut oil. For the olive oil, consider Greek instead of the more fashionable Italian, and look for pure sesame oil in oriental markets: some so-called sesame oils are actually diluted with other oils. For deep-frying, use something less dramatic (and cheaper!) such as corn oil or groundnut (peanut) oil.

Olives Bottled black and green olives keep for a very long time and are an appetizer in their own right as well as being used for garnishes or as ingredients in other dishes. Try several manufacturers' products to see which you like best. Also check mixed olives – "cocktail mix" – sold in bulk in delicatessens.

Pepper Wherever we mention "pepper" in this book, we mean freshly ground black pepper from a pepper mill, unless we specifically say otherwise.

Tuna Canned tuna (and canned salmon, and even canned sardines for that matter) can be mashed with a variety of ingredients to provide stuffings for tomatoes, peppers, eggs and *feuilletés*.

Vinegar It is quite easy to become a vinegar junkie, with dozens of different varieties. In general, balsamic vinegar is the most versatile, but you can also buy sherry vinegar; red and white wine vinegars; cider vinegar; and various flavoured vinegars such as tarragon vinegar and raspberry vinegar. With the exception of balsamic vinegar, they are not very expensive, and they all keep for a long time, so you might as well experiment with different kinds.

THE LARDER

Eggs Devilled or other stuffed eggs, scrambled eggs in a *feuilleté* or with smoked salmon, eggs as a salad, eggs as a garnish, eggs for omelettes, eggs to coat *chiles rellenos*, eggs in egg batters, egg yolks to thicken sauces – eggs are wonderfully versatile and keep for ages.

Garlic Braids look attractive and last well. Garlic powder, garlic extract and garlic salt are no substitute for garlic cloves.

Lemons Lemons (and limes) make good dressings and garnishes, can be squeezed over things, and make a wonderfully refreshing drink when mixed with fizzy water.

The Refrigerator

Butter Nothing tastes quite as rich as butter, and traditional dishes which call for butter are normally much inferior if margarine is substituted. The health benefits of most margarines are questionable anyway.

Cheese Hard cheeses, like Parmesan and Romano, keep well and can be crumbled or grated in salads, over *carpaccio*, and for all kinds of other uses. Cheeses preserved in oil keep half-way to forever. Medium cheeses like Cheddar, Mozzarella (soft and hard) and Monterey Jack are harder to keep, and grow whiskers if neglected, but form the basis of a number of other dishes. *Crème fraîche* is a useful general purpose garnish.

Fish Bottled pickled fish, in the Scandinavian style, last well and make a first-class appetizer. Home-pickled fish (page 22) are not as long-lived, but taste better.

Mayonnaise Although home-made mayonnaise is best, you can make a very acceptable alternative by buying a good quality prepared mayonnaise and then adding more extra virgin olive oil. See page 115.

Peppers and pickles Bottled hot peppers, such a *peperoncini*, make an excellent garnish; and they keep a long time in the refrigerator. Bottled mild peppers provide more visual effect than flavour, but slips of pickled red pepper are a good garnish. Other pickled vegetables such as carrots, baby sweetcorn and even mushrooms are also good for both flavour and garnish. Indian pickles and chutneys make an excellent accompaniment to *pakoras* and *samosas*.

Sausage The sort of thing that the French call *saucissons secs* (dry sausages) can be sliced thinly – preferably on the diagonal – and are available in a wide variety of very long-lived *wursts*. Dried and smoked meats and hams also keep well; after all, that is why our ancestors devised them. Other types of sausage, such as *chorizos* and *zywiecka* are more often cooked into other dishes.

The Freezer

Puff Pastry Very ordinary ingredients can rapidly be "dressed up" as a *feuilleté* with some hastily-thawed puff pastry. Frozen *filo* (phyllo) dough is also useful.

Tortillas Whether you make them yourself or buy them, they keep for ages in the freezer. They can be thawed quickly and even re-frozen if necessary.

The Garden

Even the most casual gardener should make an attempt to keep a few fresh herbs going: mint, parsley, coriander (cilantro), dill and basil. Not only do they add their own taste, but they are also a very welcome garnish. If you don't have a garden, or if you do not like gardening, consider a herb pot or a window box; and for that matter, it is increasingly easy to buy growing herbs in little plastic pots, even from supermarkets, ready for use.

Of course, there are plenty of other herbs you can grow, and you can also grow vegetables (a couple of tomato plants can be really useful); but this is not a book about gardening. It is, however, worth mentioning that flowers can make quite an ordinary meal into something special, while some garden plants such as nasturtiums (and even weeds like dandelion) can provide edible leaves for garnishes.

Chapter One

LITTLE DISHES – MOSTLY UNCOOKED

Smoked Fish

STURGEON AND LESSER CAVIARS

Caviar is the easy appetizer par excellence. If you serve it at home, you can serve sensible quantities; the tiny amounts served in restaurants are hardly worth bothering with in many cases.

TRUE STURGEON CAVIAR

250g/8 oz caviar   crusty French bread or lightly buttered toast

Serve the caviar in a pot for everyone to help themselves, eating the caviar on small pieces of bread or toast. Less than 50g/2 oz per person is cruelty to caviar lovers, and 100g/4 oz per person is not excessive. Serve chilled, but not on ice; freezing ruins caviar. No garnishes are needed. Don't worry about using horn spoons, or silver, or whatever; it really doesn't matter. Drink Champagne, sparkling wine, or well chilled vodka. In Russia, they drink sweet Champagne with caviar, and it is a surprisingly good combination.

•

You can serve salmon roe in the same way as true caviar, or in the same way as lumpfish roe, below.

LUMPFISH "CAVIAR"

100g/4 oz lumpfish roe   4 eggs, hard-boiled and halved
120ml/4 fl oz /1/2 cup double (heavy) cream

Mash the egg yolks with the cream. If you are a perfectionist, rub the egg yolks through a wire sieve first, but this is not essential. Replace the cream-and-yolk mixture in the egg whites. Garnish with the lumpfish roe. Either arrange on individual plates (two halves per person) or make one large plate. All this would be overkill with real caviar, but lumpfish roe provides the image of affluence without the expense. It also tastes good. Both black and red lumpfish roe are dyed; the natural colour is a dull tan. Serve with sparkling wine.

SMOKED FISH

Like caviar, smoked salmon is a by-word for luxury, and deservedly so. Other kinds of smoked fish, while more plebeian are nevertheless delicious and make very easy appetizers.

SMOKED SALMON (LOX)

350g/12 oz (or more!) smoked salmon, thinly sliced
thinly sliced brown bread and butter

Use Scottish salmon if you can get it, otherwise, Scandinavian or Canadian. You can even buy frozen smoked salmon. Arrange the salmon on individual plates. If you feel the need of a garnish, use soured (dairy sour) cream, fresh cream or cream cheese. Sparkling wines are a good accompaniment, or ardent spirits: straight malt whiskies or good, chilled vodkas.

•

Some fishmongers sell smoked salmon pieces or offcuts, which make a wonderful garnish (especially with scrambled eggs) at a fraction of the price of elegantly sliced smoked salmon.

•

In the United States, smoked salmon is sometimes hot-smoked, which makes for a dry, chewy fish that cannot be sliced finely; ask for lox if you want something more like the Scottish variety.

SMOKED HERRING

4-8 fillets of smoked fish or 4 whole (small) fish fresh, crusty bread and butter

horseradish saucetoast or lemon slices

Arrange the fish on individual plates. Boneless fillets or half-fillets are easiest to eat, and cost very little more than fish with the bone in. Garnish with horseradish and a lemon slice. Serve the bread or toast separately; putting the fish on the bread makes everything soggy and unpleasant. Beer, spirits or dry white wine all go well with smoked fish. Other kinds of smoked fish can be served in the same way. Again, American smoked fish can be excessively dry and chewy if you are not careful.

SMOKED TROUT

4-8 smoked trout fillets
lemon wedges

lettuce and tomato to garnish
brown bread and butter

Smoked trout is moister and flakier than most salmon, and is normally served in fillets rather than as thin slices, but it is almost equally luxurious. One small fillet per person makes an elegant starter; two large ones make quite a meal. Garnish with the lettuce, tomato and lemon wedges, with brown bread and butter on a separate plate.

FEUILLETÉ OF SCRAMBLED EGG AND SMOKED FISH

250g/8 oz frozen puff pastry
100g-250g/4-8 oz smoked fish
80g/3 oz/1/3 cup butter

12 eggs
pepper

Thaw the pastry and roll it out to about 1.5cm/1/2 in thick. Cut into four equal rectangles. Let it rest for 10 minutes before baking it in a preheated oven at 220°C/425°F/Mark 7 for about 20 minutes until puffy and golden.

•

If you are using smoked salmon (trimmings are fine), slice it into slivers. Crumble other kinds of smoked fish into small pieces.

•

Melt the butter in a heavy frying pan (skillet). Beat the eggs together. Cook them slowly in the butter, stirring constantly; this is the only way to get a really creamy texture. When the eggs are almost cooked to your taste, add the fish and distribute it well throughout the eggs.

•

Pull the "lids" off the flaky pastry and arrange the rectangles on individual plates. Pour over the eggs, add pepper to taste (the fish should add enough salt) and replace the "lids". Serve with Champagne or sparkling wine.

•

The *feuilleté* of puff pastry can be used to "dress up" almost any creamy filling, including plain scrambled eggs, or mushrooms fried in butter and then mixed with double (heavy) cream.

OLIVES IN SPICED VINEGAR

It is a matter of common observation that olives around the Mediterranean always taste better than olives anywhere else. The reason is simple: Mediterranean olives are often spiced. Two possibilities are given here, but you can experiment to create your own favourites.

200g/7 oz jar green olives, stone in
2.5ml/1/2 tsp ground cumin
2.5ml/1/2 tsp dried oregano
1.5ml/1/4 tsp crushed dried rosemary
2.5 ml/1/2 tsp dried thyme

1 bay leaf
1 clove garlic, thinly sliced
60ml/4 tbsp wine vinegar
50-120 ml/2-4 fl oz/ml/1/4-1/2 cup water

"Crack" the olives by hitting them with the flat of a large knife or cleaver; this helps the flavour to penetrate. You can score a line down one side with a knife if you prefer, going all the way to the stone: it will look neater, but it also takes longer and will not give you as good a flavour in the long run. Put everything in a jar together; add the water last, putting in just enough to cover the olives. Shake well. They will have absorbed some flavour in as little as three days, but the longer you leave them, the better. They will keep for a week or two without refrigeration, or for many weeks if refrigerated, but they taste best at room temperature.

PROSCIUTTO WITH MELON

Prosciutto crudo is the Italian for raw ham. But outside Italy 'prosciutto' means the raw, highly flavoured smoked hams which are sliced paper thin. Adding fresh melon or other fruit provides a wonderful contrast of textures and flavours.

INGREDIENTS

175-350g/6-12 oz Italian *prosciutto crudo*
1/2 small white or yellow melon
sprigs of fresh mint for garnish (optional)

Seed the melon and slice it into thin crescents. Peel each crescent; some people leave the skin on, but we find that the peeled melon is much more agreeable to eat. Divide the ham between four plates and arrange the melon in a fan on top. Garnish with sprigs of mint.

•

The precise variety of melon is a matter of choice and availability. Most melons, including the Charentais and the honeydew, are suitable.

VARIATION

Instead of melon, serve the *prosciutto* with very fresh figs. Choose green or purple figs which are ripe, but still slightly firm. Split the figs vertically (one per person) almost to the stem and gently loosen the skin near the stalk. Arrange on top of the ham.

OLIVES WITH THYME

200g/7 oz jar green olives, stone in
30ml/2 tbsp chopped fresh thyme
enough olive oil to cover (about 120ml/4 fl oz/1/2 cup)
1 clove garlic, thinly sliced (optional)

Drain the olives carefully in a colander or strainer. "Crack" them as described above. Put them back in the jar (or in another jar) with the thyme and oil, and garlic. Leave at room temperature for at least 24 hours, preferably longer. They will keep for months, provided they remain covered with oil and provided you follow two simple rules. Always fish them out with a clean teaspoon, and never return olives to the jar if they have been out for more than a few minutes. If you do refrigerate them, allow them to come to room temperature before you serve them. Otherwise the oil will be glutinous and unpleasant looking.

Prosciutto, *deliciously complimented by adding fresh fruit.*

ANTIPASTO MISTO

Antipasto misto or antipasto Italiano are what most people used to expect when they ordered "antipasti" in an Italian restaurant. Traditionally, a massive plate of salami, prosciutto, ham, olives, peppers and lots more would be brought for everyone to share; but today, a more restrained selection on individual plates would be more normal. Allow 30-50g/2 oz per person of any or all of the following.

INGREDIENTS

salami, thinly sliced (various kinds)
prosciutto, sliced paper thin
bresaola (dried beef), thinly sliced
ham, thinly sliced
smoked turkey or chicken, thinly sliced
cheese, thinly sliced or diced in
   5mm/1/4 in cubes
hard-boiled eggs, halved or quartered
canned tuna, drained
watercress

salad or garnish
olives (black or green)
peperoncini
lettuce or other crisp, raw greens
tomatoes, especially cherry tomatoes
cucumber, sliced
artichoke hearts
lemon wedges
basil sprigs

If you make an elaborate salad, dress it with a vinaigrette (page 114). If the salad is merely a garnish, leave it undressed. Serve with *grissini* (ready-made, or see page 59)

An Italian dish of mixed salami and olives.

MOZZARELLA SALADS

A staple of Italian antipasti is Mozzarella cheese combined with any number of everyday ingredients. Use either the soft Mozzarella for salads, stored in liquid, either buffalo or cow's milk, or the hard Mozzarella sold as "Mozzarella for pizza", which often works well when cooked. The latter keeps better in the refrigerator.

INSALATA CAPRESE

250 g/8 oz Mozzarella cheese
400g/14 oz firm, medium-sized tomatoes
salt and pepper

15ml/1 tbsp olive oil
fresh basil or dried oregano

Slice the Mozzarella and tomatoes and arrange in alternate slices on a plate. Season with salt and pepper and sprinkle with olive oil (a shaker is ideal). Garnish with chopped or whole fresh basil, or sprinkle with dried oregano.

•

Some people add a little sliced avocado to this, for an even more colourful combination.

MOZZARELLA WITH MELON

1/2 small Charentais or similar melon
100g/4 oz Mozzarella cheese
30-45ml/2-3 tbsp walnut oil (optional)

8 walnut halves
watercress sprigs for garnish
salt and pepper (optional)

De-seed the melon, peel it and cut it into thin slices. Arrange in a fan shape on four serving plates. Cut the Mozzarella in batons about 4cm/11/2 in long, and arrange at the base of the fan. Pour a little walnut oil over the cheese. Garnish with the walnut halves and sprigs of watercress. Season to taste.

MOZZARELLA AND BREAD

1 French or Italian loaf (*baton* or *baguette*)   250g/8oz Mozzarella cheese

Cut bread into rounds a generous 2.5cm/1 in thick. Cut the Mozzarella into slices about 1cm/1/2 in thick and rather smaller in diameter than the bread. On a bamboo skewer, arrange four or five rounds of bread and three or four rounds of Mozzarella. Push the bread tightly together so that the cheese is all but invisible. Bake (preferably on a non-stick baking tray) in a pre-heated oven at 180ºC/350ºF/Mark 4 for up to 10 minutes, or until you can see the melted cheese beginning to come out. Serve with red wine.

MOZZARELLA AND AUBERGINE (EGGPLANT)

250g/8 oz Mozzarella cheese
1-2 large purple aubergines (eggplants)
oil (preferably olive oil) for deep-frying

salt and pepper
basil for garnish

Cut the Mozzarella into thin slices about 5mm/1/2 in thick. Cut the aubergine into rounds 1cm/1/2 in thick. In hot oil about 180º-190ºC/350º-375ºF, fry the aubergine for 3-5 minutes until it is brown. While it is still piping hot, arrange the aubergine and Mozzarella in alternate slices on individual serving plates. Season with salt and pepper and garnish with basil.

BRUSCHETTA

Bruschetta – singed bread – in Roman dialect – is one of the quickest, easiest and best-tasting bread appetizers you can make. Even the most ordinary supermarket French loaf is transformed. It does not even matter if the bread is a bit stale.

INGREDIENTS

8-12 slices French or Italian bread, about 2cm/3/4 in thick
120ml/4 fl oz/1/2 cup olive oil
2 small to medium tomatoes

1-2 large cloves garlic
12 fresh basil leaves
salt and pepper (optional)

Preheat the oven to 200°C/400°F/Mark 6. Put the slices of bread on a baking sheet and bake for 10 minutes or until golden brown; neither the time nor the oven temperature is very critical.

•

Pour the olive oil into a small dish or deep saucer. Slice the tomatoes.

•

Once the bread is cool enough to handle, rub the top surface with the garlic; the bread will rasp off a small amount of the garlic. Next, dip the bread momentarily in the oil; a second or less on each side. Leaving it longer will soak up more oil and make the *bruschetta* too oily for some tastes.

•

Finally sandwich a basil leaf under a slice of tomato placed on top, or sprinkle chopped basil on the tomato. Add salt and pepper if you like.

PALM HEART AND ARTICHOKE SALAD

Canned or bottled palm hearts and artichoke hearts keep indefinitely but are sufficiently exotic and luxurious to be served as an unusual appetizer without apology at a few minutes notice.

INGREDIENTS

1 x 300-450g/12-15 oz can or bottle palm hearts
1 x 300-450g/12-15 oz can or bottle artichoke hearts
30ml/2 tbsp walnut oil
10ml/2 tsp sherry or balsamic vinegar
1/4 tsp dry mustard

Drain the palm hearts and rinse them carefully; they will taste a little harsh and astringent otherwise. If the artichoke hearts are in oil, merely drain them, but if they are in water, wash and drain them well.

•

Cut the palm hearts into sections up to 5cm/2 in long; halve or quarter the artichoke hearts. Mix the two together.

•

Mix the oil, vinegar and mustard to make a vinaigrette – you can of course use other vinaigrettes, page 114, to taste – and dress the vegetables with this. Serve at room temperature.

ROLLMOPS AND OTHER PICKLED FISH

Commercially made pickled fish are as quick and easy to serve as caviar and smoked salmon, but they cost a lot less and are easier to store. Most of the bottled varieties will last for weeks or months in the refrigerator, and can be served straight from the jar.

SERVING PICKLED FISH

1 small loaf brown or black rye bread
1 small loaf pumpernickel
250g/1 cup/8 oz butter
12-18 pickled fish fillets, various kinds

Slice the bread thinly, butter it generously, and serve it separately from the pickled fish. Accompany with beer and ardent spirits: aquavit, schnapps or vodka, or even Scotch.

•

Although there is little point in trying to make the more exotic forms of pickled fish, the ones that are preserved with soured (dairy sour) cream and so forth, it is fun to make your own rollmops from time to time. The recipe given below is for four people, but you might do better to make a double or triple recipe for a party with friends. All-male parties can shift astonishing amounts of rollmops.

BASIC ROLLMOPS

12 juniper berries
12 cloves
24 black peppercorns
1 litre/1 3/4 pts/4 1/4 cups vinegar
2 white onions
8 fresh herring fillets

Partially flatten the spices with the side of a cleaver or a heavy knife. Add them to the vinegar and heat rapidly to boiling point in a stainless steel or enamel pan. Do not use an aluminium pan as the vinegar will react with it. As soon as it begins to boil, cool it down again by placing the pan in a bowl of cold water. Leave the window open if you can: the smell of hot vinegar can be overwhelming.

•

Chop the onions, or cut them into half-rings. Roll the fish fillets around the onions, and secure them with a cocktail stick (toothpick). In a glass vessel, cover the rollmops with the cold vinegar, and leave to marinate in the refrigerator for at least 3 days and preferably twice as long.

VARIATIONS

Spread the fish fillet with prepared mustard (French, English or German) before you roll it, or include a small gherkin along with the onions in the middle.

FISH ZAKUSKI

Fish, normally served on bite-sized pieces of rye bread or heavy Russian khleb, *are an essential part of* zakuski, *the elaborate Russian* hors d'oeuvres *which frequently constitute a meal in their own right. They are commonly served with caviar (page 14), potato salads (page 52), beet and walnut salad (page 32), pickled mushrooms or mushrooms à la Grècque (page 28), and chicken salads. No quantities are given below because you can make as much or as little as you want, depending on availability and inclination.*

INGREDIENTS

light rye bread
dark rye bread
butter
smoked salmon (trimmings are fine)
smoked trout
smoked mackerel
canned small fish (sild, sardines, etc.)
lumpfish or true caviar or salmon roe
pickled fish
fresh dill
dill sauce (see below)
gherkins for garnish

Cut the thinly sliced bread into bite-sized pieces, at most 5cm/2 in square. Butter generously. Place a morsel of fish or a spoonful of caviar on each piece of bread; the idea is that the whole thing should be consumed at a single bite. Garnish with fresh dill, soured (dairy sour) cream (or *crème fraîche, smetana* or similar), or dill sauce. Serve with well-chilled vodka and Champagne – sweet Champagne if you want to be authentically Russian.

DILL SAUCE

250ml/8 fl oz//1 cup full cream yoghurt (Greek-style is excellent)
120ml/4 fl oz/1/2 cup mayonnaise (page 115)
5ml/1 tsp lemon juice
30ml/2 tbsp chopped fresh tarragon, or 10ml/2 tsp dried
30ml/2 tbsp chopped fresh dill

The precise size of your measuring cup is not important; what is important is the 2:1 proportion of yoghurt to mayonnaise. Finely chop the herbs, then mix everything together. This is a delicious sauce which keeps for many days in the refrigerator, improving all the time.

BAGNA CAUDA

Bagna cauda means literally "hot bath", and this Italian dish is something between a dip and a fondue. The attraction lies in the contrasts between the hot sauce with its complex flavours, and the freshness and simplicity of the vegetables you dip into it.

INGREDIENTS

1 50g/2 oz can anchovies
1 small onion, finely chopped
1 clove garlic, finely chopped (optional)
30g/1 oz/2 tbsp butter
150ml/5 fl oz/2/3 cup olive oil
Fresh vegetables (*crudités*) for dipping)

Chop the anchovies finely and then pound them in a mortar; or purée in a liquidizer. Melt the butter in a small, heavy saucepan. Gently fry the onion and garlic until they are golden and soft. Add the oil and anchovies. Warm almost to boiling point, but do not allow mixture to boil.

•

Traditionally, this is served either in the vessel in which it is cooked or in a small purpose-made earthenware dish. A fondue dish will do, but take care not to over-heat the dip. Use whatever crudités you like or can get: traditional choices include cardoons and chicory (endive), but you can use carrot sticks, pieces of cucumber, spring onions (scallions) and anything else. The longer the sauce stews lazily away in the dish, the better it will taste. Serve with a light, slightly chilled white or red wine; white *vinho verde* is good.

VARIATIONS

The only fixed points are the anchovies, the onions and the butter. *Bagna cauda* can be made with more butter, or even with cream, and the oil can be reduced or even omitted. The quantities given above are half those given in most Italian cookery books, but will still be more than adequate for four people.

CRUDITÉS

Crudités *are nothing more or less than raw vegetables served with a dip. The most usual dips are mayonnaise or* aïoli *(garlic mayonnaise), made according to the recipes on page 115, but you can also use flavoured vinaigrettes (page 114); Mexican bean dip (page 70); hummus or taramasalata (page 48); soured (dairy sour) cream or yoghurt, with or without such additions as chopped chives or curry powder; or the anchovy dip below.* Bagna cauda *(page 24) is a hot dip, ideal in the winter.*

THE VEGETABLES

Any or all of the following:
4 sticks celery
2 medium-sized carrots
8 spring onions (scallions)
1 bell pepper
1 cucumber
1/2 cauliflower
2 courgettes (zucchini)
1 bulb fennel
8 mushrooms
8 ears baby sweet corn (up to 7.5cm/3 in long)
8-12 radishes
4 cardoons
8 cherry tomatoes

Cut the celery into sticks 10-15cm/4-6 in long and up to 1cm/1/2 in square. Peel or scrape the carrots and quarter them lengthways. Peel the outer skins off the spring onions (scallions) and cut off the roots. De-seed the bell pepper (red, yellow, orange or green) and slice into strips from top to bottom. Partially or fully peel the cucumber and cut into sections 10-15cm/4-6 in long. Quarter each section lengthways. Break the cauliflower (or broccoli) into florets. Quarter the courgettes (zucchini) lengthways. Slice the fennel. Slice the mushrooms if necessary.

COLD ANCHOVY SAUCE

6-8 anchovy fillets
2 cloves garlic (optional)
a little milk (to soak the anchovies)
15ml/1 tbsp capers
100ml/3 1/2 fl oz/scant 1/2 cup olive oil
juice of 1/2 lemon
black pepper to taste

This is the classic French dip for *crudités*. Soak the anchovies in milk for 30 minutes to remove as much salt as possible (you can omit this step if you are not too fussy). Drain. Place in a blender or pestle and mortar and reduce to a purée. Add the garlic if you are using it, and then add the other ingredients as soon as the anchovy is reasonably finely chopped. Even people who do not like anchovies often like this dip, especially if you neglect to tell them what is in it.

AUBERGINE "CAVIAR"

Found throughout south-eastern Europe and into Russia and Georgia, aubergine (eggplant)
"caviar" does not bear very much resemblance to anything fishy but it is delicious in its own right.

INGREDIENTS

1 large aubergine (eggplant)
1 large mild onion
2-4 cloves garlic
1 large tomato
up to 175ml/6 fl oz/3/4 cup extra virgin olive oil
pitta bread for dipping

Puncture the aubergine a few times with a fork, and bake it in a preheated oven at 200°C/400°F/Mark 6, for about 1 hour until it is blackened and wrinkled and feels soft to the touch. Peel it while it is still hot – you may burn your fingers a little, but it is much quicker and easier this way.

•

Chop the onion and garlic finely. Dice the aubergine (eggplant). Peel the tomato (pour boiling water over the top to loosen the skin) and chop.

•

Working on a large board, chop all the ingredients together repeatedly. You may lose a little moisture over the edge at first; have some kitchen roll handy, or work on the draining board. When everything is fairly finely chopped, start adding the oil and chopping that into the mixture: it is surprising how it all holds together. The amount of oil you need will depend on the moistness of the other ingredients and your own taste. Serve at room temperature, with toasted pitta bread for dipping. It can be made in advance, even the day before, and stored in the refrigerator, but allow it to reach room temperature before serving.

MUSHROOMS
À LA GRÈCQUE

À la Grècque is a French term which accurately describes a typical Greek way of cooking, in a mixture of oil, lemon juice and water. Mushrooms are the most usual thing to cook, but other vegetables can be treated the same way. They can be served hot or (more usually) at room temperature – but not chilled, when they are rather unpleasant.

INGREDIENTS

500g/1 lb button mushrooms
60ml/4 tbsp olive oil
juice of 1/2 lemon
120ml/4 fl oz/1/2 cup water
salt and pepper

Wash, clean and trim the mushrooms as necessary. Put all the ingredients into a fairly deep pan, seasoning them heavily. Bring to the boil, then reduce the heat and cover the pan. The lid should not be too tight-fitting: you want to lose a certain amount of moisture by evaporation. The mushrooms are cooked when most of the water has gone, and they are sitting in a thin layer of oil and mushroom juice on the bottom of the pan.

•

Serve hot or at room temperature, or store in a jar in the refrigerator with whatever cooking liquid remains. They will keep for many days, but they must be allowed to come to room temperature before serving.

CARPACCIO

Anyone who likes steak tartare should love carpaccio. It is very thinly sliced raw beef, served in a variety of ways throughout Italy: plain or marinated, with or without mayonnaise, more or less garnished.

INGREDIENTS

750g/1 1/2 lb lean beef
100-150g/4-5 oz Romano or Parmesan cheese
60-90ml/4-6 tbsp olive oil
juice of 2 lemons or 3 limes
black pepper

Any meat which would make a good roast will also make good *carpaccio*: topside, for example, is fine. Remove all fat or gristle, so that only good pink meat is left. Chill until almost (but not quite) frozen – this makes it easiest to slice – and slice as thinly as possible with a *very* sharp knife or rotary food-slicer. Cutting the meat thinly enough is the only difficult part about this recipe. There will be a certain amount of wastage, including the last bit of meat that you cannot slice, so you should end up with 100-150g/4-5 oz of thinly sliced meat per person.

•

Arrange on individual plates. With a knife, shave the cheese in flakes on to the meat. Serve with olive oil and lemon or lime juice for drizzling over the meat, and freshly grated black pepper.

MARINATED CARPACCIO

You can marinate the beef before you serve it (but after you slice it) in a mixture of lemon juice and olive oil in about equal parts. The longer you leave it in the marinade, the more tender it will be but the less pronounced the flavour will be. Marinating time can range from 15 minutes to overnight; if you leave it overnight, the meat will be blanched as if it is cooked.

CARPACCIO WITH MAYONNAISE

If you serve it with mayonnaise, add 45ml/2 tbsp of cream and about 2.5ml/1/2 tsp mustard to 250ml/8 fl oz/1 cup of mayonnaise – the proportions are not very critical – mix well, and lay the mayonnaise in stripes on top of the meat.

GARNISHES AND ACCOMPANIMENTS

Carpaccio is not normally garnished at all, except as described above, but you can serve it on a bed of rocket leaves or similar salad; or with cornichons or capers; or even with a quartered hard-boiled egg.

•

Bread or bread sticks would be a normal accompaniment. To drink, a sparkling wine or a very dry white wine is best, but a medium-bodied red wine is good, too.

CHICKEN AND AVOCADO SALAD

This is apparently a Californian recipe, though it may originally have been Mexican. It is surprisingly rich: a quantity which looks quite inadequate for four people will turn out to be more than enough.

INGREDIENTS

1 small chicken or two large chicken breasts or half a cold chicken
2 small onions
1 bay leaf
12 black peppercorns
salt
4 medium-to-large avocados
50g/2 oz black olives
75g/3 oz almonds or hazelnuts (optional)
120ml/4 fl oz/1/2 cup mayonnaise (page 115)
crusty bread and butter
cayenne pepper

Boil the chicken with the onions, bay leaf and peppercorns, with salt to taste: Let it cool in the stock, then bone it and dice it in 1 cm/1/2 in cubes. A whole small chicken will give the best flavour, but a couple of boiled chicken breasts is easier and less messy. Fresh left-over chicken is also a good candidate. You should end up with just under 500g/1 lb of meat.

•

Peel and dice the avocados. Pit the olives, and slice into rings – or use sliced olives. If you are using nuts, reserve a few to grate over the top. Mix everything gently: the avocados break up and lose their shape otherwise. Sprinkle cayenne pepper over the top.

•

Serve with crusty bread and almost any wine or beer – it is excellent with a light, well-chilled *rosé*.

BEET AND WALNUT SALAD

This is a traditional Russian salad, offered as part of zakuski. *It looks nondescript, but tastes very good and is surprisingly rich, because of the cream.*

INGREDIENTS

1-2 cloves garlic
120ml/4 fl oz/1/2 cup soured (dairy sour) cream
250g/8 oz cooked, peeled beetroot (red beets)
100g/4 oz chopped walnuts
crusty bread
butter

Peel and crush the garlic and mix it with the soured (dairy sour) cream. Dice the beetroot finely – 5mm/1/2 in cubes are fine – and mix it with the walnuts and the soured (dairy sour) cream. Chill for several hours to allow the garlic flavour to permeate all through the salad. Serve with other *zakuski*, and crusty bread and butter.

VARIATIONS

The proportion of beetroot to walnuts is not at all critical, and instead of the soured cream you can use *crème fraîche* or *crema Mexicana* (which is probably closest to Russian soured cream) or even thick Greek-style yoghurt. You can even use pickled beetroot, provided the vinegar flavour is not too pronounced, though the earthy taste of freshly cooked beetroot is preferable.

Chapter Two

LITTLE SIMPLY COOKED DISHES

Roasted Pepper Salad

ARTICHOKES

Artichokes may be slightly hard work to eat, pulling off each leaf in turn and stripping the meaty part from it with your teeth, but they are wonderfully easy to cook. For some reason many people have never tried them, but they make a superb appetizer. They are also very good cold with vinaigrette for picnics.

INGREDIENTS

4 globe artichokes
water for steaming
melted butter or mayonnaise (page 115) for dipping

Wash the artichokes; pull off any tough or damaged outer leaves, and trim off the stem at the base so that the artichoke sits upright. Some people trim off the prickles on the leaves, and remove the hairy inedible "choke" which covers the delicious base of the vegetable, but it is easier (and just as acceptable) to leave these chores for your guests.

•

On a rack, in a saucepan or in a purpose-made steamer, steam the artichokes in a closed pan for anything from 15 to 45 minutes. The British like their artichokes under-done, but most Europeans cook them thoroughly.

•

As alternatives to melted butter or mayonnaise, try *aïoli* (page 115) or the dipping sauce for crudités (page 26). Do not forget to provide a plate for the leaves and "chokes".

FRIED CHEESE

You can deep-fry almost any reasonably solid cheese. The only trick lies in coating it so it will not leak all over the frying pan. The technique below will prevent problems,

DEEP-FRIED CAMEMBERT

1 x 250g/8oz Camembert cheese
1 large or 2 small eggs
50g/2 oz/1/2 cup plain (all-purpose) flour
100g/4 oz/1 cup dried breadcrumbs
oil for deep-frying
cranberry sauce for garnish

Leave the cheese in the refrigerator for at least 1 hour before you attempt to fry it. Beat the egg(s). Put the flour on one plate, and the breadcrumbs on another.

•

Cut the cheese into eighths (quarter it, and halve each quarter). Coat each segment evenly with flour, then with beaten egg, then with breadcrumbs.

•

Heat the oil to 190°C/375°F. Deep-fry the coated cheese for 3-5 minutes or until a deep golden brown. Keep a close eye on it for leaks: as soon as any piece shows any sign of leaking, the cheese is cooked. Serve with cranberry sauce.

FRIED MOZZARELLA

250g/8 oz Mozzarella cheese
1 large or 2 small eggs
100g/4 oz/1 cup dried breadcrumbs
50g/2 oz/1/2 cup plain (all-purpose) flour
oil for deep-frying

Prepare as for deep-fried Camembert. Serve with home-made tomato sauce (page 87) or tomato ketchup.

WELSH RAREBIT

Welsh rarebit is much more than just cheese on toast. It is a mixture of good cheese and strong beer, and has considerably more flavour and character than cheese alone.

INGREDIENTS

4 slices bread
butter
250g/8 oz mature Cheddar or other strong cheese
175ml/6 fl oz/3/4 cup strong ale
15ml/1tbsp dry English mustard
pepper to taste

Toast the bread and butter it. Put the pieces on individual ovenproof plates. Grate the cheese, and put it in a heavy saucepan with the beer, mustard and pepper. Melt all the ingredients together until they form a smooth paste, then pour the paste on to the toast: it may be thinner than you expect. Brown under the grill (broiler) for 3-4 minutes.

BROCCOLI AND SESAME

Sesame oil and sesame seeds make an unusual combination with boiled broccoli. This is said to be a Szechuan dish, though we have never verified its authenticity. It can be served as a vegetable accompanying another dish, or (as here) as a light but surprisingly tasty and filling dish in its own right.

INGREDIENTS

750g/1 1/2 lb broccoli
30ml/2 tbsp sesame seeds
2 cloves garlic
30ml/2 tbsp sesame oil

15ml/1tbsp soy sauce
15g/1/2 oz fresh ginger root (optional)
2 spring onions (scallions) (optional)

Break the broccoli into bite-sized pieces, florets and stems alike. Boil it in plenty of salted water for 3-5 minutes until it is soft. As soon as the colour is bright green, it is ready. Drain it well.

•

Meanwhile, toast the sesame seeds in a heavy iron pan, or in an oven preheated to 190°C/375°F/Mark 5 until they are just beginning to turn golden brown. Do not cook them too hot or too long, or they will burn and pop.

•

Slice the garlic very thinly. Mix with the oil and soy sauce (shaking them together in a jam jar is very effective). If you are using ginger root, crush this into the mixture, using a garlic press. Finely chop the spring onions (scallions) and add them to the dressing if you use them; we usually do not. Pour the dressing over the broccoli, and toss lightly, taking care not to break up the broccoli unduly. Sprinkle the toasted sesame seeds over the top.

•

Serve warm or at room temperature; it is not very good if you chill it. It can be stored overnight in the refrigerator, and may be even better next day if it is allowed to reach room temperature before serving.

ANCHOVY AND CREAM SAVOURY

"Savouries", served at the end of a meal were once an essential component of any grand banquet. In a less indulgent age, dishes such as this late-Victorian treat make a luxurious snack or can be served with other small dishes.

INGREDIENTS

4 slices white bread, about 1cm/1/2 in thick
30g/1 oz/2 tbsp butter
8-12 anchovy fillets
120ml/4 fl oz/1/2 cup clotted cream or thick double (very heavy) cream, well chilled

If you want to reduce the intensity of the flavour of the anchovies as well as reducing the salt somewhat, drain them well and soak them in milk for 30 minutes. You can also use them straight from the can, merely drained and patted dry with a paper towel.

•

With a 10cm/4 in biscuit-cutter (cookie-cutter), cut rounds from the centres of the slices of white bread. The size is not critical.

•

Heat the butter in a frying pan (skillet). When it is good and hot, fry each round of bread on both sides. They should be crisp and golden and should need little or no draining.

•

Put them on individual plates. Drape 2-3 anchovy fillets across the fried bread, and top with a large spoonful of cream. Serve immediately: they go soggy in a few minutes. The contrast of textures and flavours when they are served fresh is, however, explosive.

•

The best cream to use is Cornish (or failing that, Devon) clotted dream, but if you cannot get that, you need a cream that is solid enough not to melt. If you cannot stand a heavy spoon up in it, then it is too thin. You can get away with *crème fraîche* but it is a meagre substitute.

BEAN SALADS

Whether you use fresh, dried or even canned beans, there are all kinds of bean salads which are quick and easy to make and which usually cost next to nothing.

French Bean Salad

500g/1 lb young French or string beans (*haricot verts*)
6 spring onions (scallions)
120ml/4 oz/1/2 cup vinaigrette (page 114)
5-10ml/1-2 tsp salt

Bring a large pan of lightly salted water to the boil. The beans should be young enough to need no trimming; wash them only. Boil for 1-2 minutes so that they are still slightly crisp. Drain carefully, and pat dry with a paper towel. Cut each bean in half (except the smallest ones) and leave to cool. Mix in the spring onions (scallions) and dress with vinaigrette. Use a flavoured vinaigrette (with anchovy, perhaps) if you like.

Hot Bean and Almond Salad

350g/12 oz mature green beans
80g/3 oz/1/3 cup butter
100g/4 oz/1 cup nibbed or flaked almonds

Top and tail the beans, and remove the strings. Slice the beans diagonally into about four pieces each.

•

Fry the almonds in the butter until they are beginning to brown. Add the beans and continue to cook until the beans are to your taste – anything from 3-10 minutes, depending on the age and tenderness of the beans. Serve hot.

Butter Bean Salad

250g/8oz dried butter beans or 1 x 400g/14 oz can
30-60ml/2-4 tbsp olive oil
12 fresh basil leaves
1 small red onion or 1 large shallot
cubed feta cheese (optional)
anchovy fillets (optional)
lemon slices (optional)
salt and black pepper

Pick over the dried beans carefully. Soak for 8-12 hours, and boil (without salt) until tender; anything from 30-60 minutes, depending on the beans. Drain and let cool. If you are using canned beans, rinse them in a colander.

•

Place the beans on individual plates. Drizzle olive oil over the beans. Chop most of the basil, reserving a few leaves for garnish, and sprinkle over the beans. Slice the onion or shallot very thinly and use as a garnish with feta, anchovy fillets, and a slice of lemon, as desired. Season to taste.

CANNED BEAN SALAD

1 x 400g/14 oz can cut green beans
1 x 400g/14 oz can yellow (wax) beans
15ml/1 tbsp sesame seeds
15ml/1 tbsp sesame oil

Rinse the beans under the tap and drain them thoroughly: leave them in a
colander for a few minutes, shaking them occasionally.

•

Toast the sesame seeds in an iron frying pan (skillet) or in the oven until lightly
brown. Mix the beans, toss them a couple of times in the oil and sprinkle the
sesame seeds over the top.

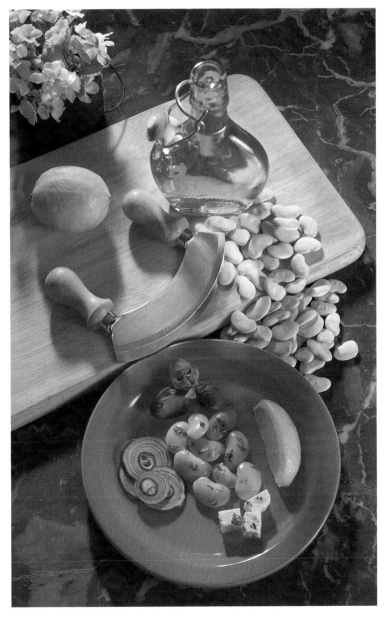

FENNEL SALADS

Fennel can be used raw or cooked in salads, and no fennel salad takes long to make. You can ring the changes by experimenting with your own favourite ingredients.

RAW FENNEL, RICE AND EGGS SALAD

100g/4 oz/1/2 cup long-grain rice
1 bulb fennel
1 small red onion
4 small tomatoes

2 hard-boiled eggs
12 black olives
120ml/4 fl oz/1/2 cup vinaigrette
(page 114)

Boil the rice until just tender then drain and leave to cool. Wash the fennel well and slice thinly. Thinly slice the onion and quarter the tomatoes. Halve or quarter the eggs. Pit the olives.

•

Toss the rice with the vinaigrette – work quickly, or some parts will be soggy and other parts uncoated – and place in a serving bowl. Place all the other ingredients on top. Serve at room temperature or chilled.

RAW FENNEL, CHEESE AND GREEN OLIVES

2 bulbs fennel
100g/4 oz cheese (Greek feta or Italian Mozzarella or Provolone)
100g/4 oz green olives
60ml/4 tbsp vinaigrette (page 114)
fresh dill for garnish

Wash the fennel and slice it thinly. Cut the cheese into 5mm/1/2 in cubes and stone (pit) the olives. Mix together all ingredients, toss in the vinaigrette and garnish with fresh dill. This is an Italian recipe, and normally would use Mozzarella or Provolone, but we like it with Greek feta cheese.

COOKED FENNEL AND DOLCELATTE

3 bulbs fennel
15ml/1 tbsp fennel seeds
60ml/4 tbsp olive oil
juice of 1/2 lemon

1/8 teaspoon sugar (optional)
Pepper and salt to taste
100g/4 oz/ Dolcelatte cheese

If the fennel comes with its green, feathery tops, trim them off and chop them to use for garnish. Plunge the bulbs into boiling water for 5 minutes, remove with a slotted spoon, and cool rapidly by running under cold water. Leave to drain well.

•

Lightly crush the fennel seeds, then heat them in a dry pan (or in a preheated oven) for a few minutes to brown and to release the aroma. Remove from the heat and add the oil, lemon juice, sugar and seasonings.

•

Slice the fennel thinly and arrange on a plate or shallow serving dish and pour over the dressing. Crumble the cheese on top and then add the chopped tops. Leave for at least 20 minutes for the flavours to marry, then toss briefly before serving.

ROSBIF MAYO

Rosbif Mayo – roast beef with mayonnaise – is a fine old French hors d' oeuvres *with a fine old approximation to an English spelling. For once, the quantities here are for six: you cannot decently roast a piece of beef that is much smaller.*

INGREDIENTS (SERVES 6)

1kg/2 lb silverside, topside or similar lean beef
250ml/8 fl oz/1 cup mayonnaise (page 115)
capers and cornichons to garnish

The beef must be lean, but with a thin layer of fat on the outside. A good butcher will roll an appropriate cut for you if you explain what you are doing. A couple of hours (or more) before you cook it, take it out of the refrigerator and allow it to come to room temperature. Preheat the oven to 225°C/425°F/Mark 7, and cook the meat for 15 minutes: it will smoke a lot and may mess the oven up a little. Fifteen minutes is for really rare French-style beef; give it 20 minutes if you prefer it a bit better done.

•

Let it cool, which takes and hour or so; slice thinly; garnish with about half the mayonnaise, half a dozen capers per person, and one or two cornichons (small, salty pickled gherkins) per person. Put the remaining mayonnaise in a bowl for people to help themselves if they want more.

•

In practice, four carnivores can demolish this amount of meat quite easily: it is only 250g/8 oz per person uncooked, and maybe 175-200g/6-7 oz cooked. In polite company, though, six or even eight servings might be more appropriate.

STUFFED TOMATOES

Stuffed tomatoes are a bit like Kipling's observation on tribal lays: "There are nine and sixty ways
of constructing tribal lays, and – every – single – one – of – them – is – right." The suggestions
below are merely a starting point.

THE TOMATOES

8 tomatoes (2 per person)

Choose tomatoes that are both firm and ripe – a combination not always found.
Ideally, they should be about 7-8cm/3 in in diameter: with significantly bigger
tomatoes, allow one per person. Instead of just slicing the tops off, make "crowns"
with a sharp, pointed knife. At the equator, stick the knife in at 45 degrees to the
equator to pierce the tomato somewhat beyond the core. Pull the knife out; turn
through 90 degrees; repeat, so that the two cuts meet in a vee. Work your way
around the tomato until you can pull the top off. Remove the pulp, and either
discard it or eat it – cook's perks!

•

The following fillings are in quantities to fill four tomatoes generously, so you will
need two fillings (or a double recipe of one filling) to fill all eight. Of course, a lot
depends on the size of the tomatoes, and on how well you remove the pulp.

COTTAGE CHEESE FILLING

300g.10 oz cottage cheese   a few leaves of fresh mint (optional)
small bunch of fresh chives

Chop the chives and the mint leaves, reserving a few leaves and pieces of chive for
garnish. Mix all the ingredients together. Fills four hollowed tomatoes.

TUNA AND MAYONNAISE FILLING

1 x 175g/6 oz can tuna   5ml/1 tsp capers
1 hardboiled egg   120 ml/4 fl oz/1/2 cup mayonnaise (page 115)

Drain and flake the tuna using a fork. Chop the hard-boiled egg. If the capers are
large, chop them too. Mix all the ingredients together and stuff the tomatoes. Fills
four hollowed tomatoes.

TUNA AND BEETROOT FILLING

1 x 175g/6 oz can tuna
3-4 cooked baby beetroot (red beet) about 100g/4 oz
60ml/4 tbsp soured (dairy sour) cream

Drain and flake the tuna, Dice the beetroot finely. Mix the tuna and beetroot. Top
with a teaspoonful of soured (dairy sour) cream. Fills four hollowed tomatoes.

EGG AND MAYONNAISE FILLING

3 hard-boiled eggs
120ml/4 fl oz/1/2 cup mayonnaise (page 115)
30ml/2 tbsp chopped fresh basil, plus leaves for garnish

Chop the eggs and mix with the mayonnaise and basil. Fill the tomatoes. Garnish
with the remaining basil leaves. Fills four hollowed tomatoes.

PINEAPPLE FILLING

1/2 fresh pineapple

a handful of chopped mixed nuts

120ml/4 fl oz/1/2 cup mayonnaise (page 115)

salt and pepper

Ideally, use plum tomatoes, and slice them in half lengthways. Remove the seeds, sprinkle the shells with salt and pepper, and leave upside down to purge for 30 minutes. Peel the pineapple, and cut the flesh into small pieces. Mix with the nuts, in the proportion of two-thirds pineapple to one-third nuts. Put the mixture in the tomatoes and top with mayonnaise. This is a refreshing dish in the summer.

BRAISED FENNEL

Braised fennel makes a superb vegetarian dish, and it is not necessary actually to braise it. By combining boiling and frying, you can prepare it in 20 minutes or so.

INGREDIENTS

4 large bulbs fennel
30ml/2 tbsp olive oil
30ml/2 tbsp butter

Boil the fennel in salted water until it is just cooked – typically for 10-12 minutes. Drain well. If they are very thick, slice each bulb in half from top to bottom through the thin dimension.

•

Heat the oil and butter together over a moderate heat in a heavy frying pan (skillet), and fry both sides of each piece for up to 5 minutes a side or until it looks wilted. Exactly how much you cook it is a matter of personal taste; one of us likes it barely cooked, almost like raw celery, and the other likes it cooked until it is nearly mushy.

•

Serve immediately, hot or warm, with a crisp white wine. We have never found anything that makes a good garnish, though some people like to squeeze a little lemon juice over it.

ROASTED PEPPER SALADS

Blistering peppers (bell peppers) to make a salad is a tedious, wrist-aching business, but it makes a wonderfully appetizing smell and the end result is worth the effort. Besides, it does not really take all that long, just ten minutes or so.

INGREDIENTS

3 peppers (bell peppers)
30g/1 oz anchovies in oil
50g/2 oz feta cheese, cubed

Drain the anchovies, and if you want to reduce the intensity of the flavour and remove some of the salt, soak them in milk for 30 minutes.

•

Blister the peppers over a gas flame until the skin is blackened over at least two-thirds of its area. As each pepper is finished, put it in a paper or plastic bag, or in a pot with a close fitting lid. After they have rested for a few minutes, the skin should scrape off easily. Do not worry if you cannot get all of it off, because a few pieces here and there will not matter. Red peppers taste sweetest: yellow, orange and green peppers add visual variety.

•

Quarter the peppers and remove the seeds. Arrange three pepper quarters on each plate. Place a fillet of anchovy on each quarter, and garnish with a few cubes of feta; we use the sort which is preserved in oil with herbs (page 118).

•

Serve at room temperature, *not* chilled, preferably with bread sticks (page 59).

VARIATIONS

You can bake the sliced peppers after they have been roasted – it will make them more tender – and you can either bake them with Mozzarella cheese (which will, of course, melt) or you can interleave them with finely sliced Mozzarella after they have cooled.

PASTA SALADS

Pasta absorbs a lot of flavour, so pasta salads must not be bland and dull. The key to making them interesting is to be generous with strongly flavoured ingredients, especially fresh herbs.

BASIC PASTA SALAD

250g/8 oz uncooked pasta (macaroni, shells or other shapes)
60ml/4 tbsp strongly flavoured olive oil
1 shallot or 4 spring onions (scallions) (optional)
5ml/1 tbsp finely chopped fresh basil
salt and black pepper

Boil the pasta in plenty of salted water, preferably with a little olive oil added, until it is just cooked: as the Italians say, *al dente*. While it is cooking, chop the shallot or spring onions (scallions). Drain the pasta, and before it is fully cool, add the oil, the chopped herbs and the onions, and season to taste. Serve with other *antipasti*, and plenty of robust red wine.

CHICKEN PASTA SALAD

250g/8 oz uncooked pasta (macaroni, shells or other shapes)
250g/8 oz cooked chicken
30g/1 oz black olives
1-2 hot red chilli peppers (optional)
4 spring onions (scallions)
120ml/4 fl oz/1/2 cup mayonnaise (page 115)
2.5ml/1/2 tsp finely chopped fresh thyme
2.5ml/1/2 tsp finely chopped fresh oregano
salt and black pepper
lettuce and tomatoes for garnish
lemon wedges (optional)

Boil the pasta as described above. Drain it and let it cool. Dice the chicken, not too finely. Skinless chicken breasts are fine, but so is any other chicken meat. Stone (pit) the olives and slice them in rings, or use stoned olives. De-seed the chilli peppers and chop them finely. Chop the spring onions (scallions). Mix all the ingredients together. Season, using plenty of black pepper. Garnish with lettuce and tomato and wedges of lemon. Serve with a fresh white wine.

VARIATIONS

The variations are limited only by your imagination. Use coloured or flavoured pasta. Make a tuna and pasta salad: pasta, tuna and mayonnaise, with freshly chopped tarragon. Try chicken and asparagus and pasta – this needs no herbs. Add grated hard cheese (such as Parmesan) to the basic pasta salad above, or cubes of feta in oil (page 118) to most pasta salads. Add chopped or sliced hard-boiled eggs to almost any pasta salad. Needless to say, proportions are rarely critical. The main things to watch are first, not to add too much mayonnaise – this can make for a cloying salad – and second, to be generous with the strong flavours such as herbs, cheese, black olives and rich extra virgin olive oil.

GREEK DIPS

Taramasalata, hummus and tzatziki, eaten with pitta bread, are classic Mediterranean mezé or mezedes – but they are also a light meal in themselves. You can buy all three ready-made, but the home-made versions of hummus and tzatziki are incomparably better, and only the very best store-bought taramasalata is any good.

TARAMASALATA

6 thin slices white bread
1/2 Spanish onion or 1 large shallot (optional)
1-2 cloves garlic
100g/4 oz smoked grey mullet roe or smoked cod's roe
juice of 1 lemon
250ml/8 fl oz/1 cup olive oil
olives and chopped fresh parsley for garnish

Trim the crusts and soak the bread in water. Squeeze reasonably dry; you don't want it running with water, but you don't want a tight, sticky lump either.

•

Blend the onion or shallot and garlic in a liquidizer, and add the roe and bread. With the liquidizer running, add the oil and lemon alternately; the aim is a smooth paste. This is a strongly flavoured taramasalata, and you may want to add more bread, in which case increase the oil and lemon juice proportionately. Garnish with olives and chopped parsley.

HUMMUS

250g/8 oz dried chickpeas (garbanzo beans) or 1 x 250g/8 oz can
1-3 cloves garlic
up to 150ml/1/2 pt/2/3 cup extra virgin olive oil
juice of 1/2 lemon
salt to taste (up to 5ml/1 tsp)
black olives for garnish, pitted
pitta bread for dipping

Soak the chickpeas for 6-12 hours. Drain, then boil them in unsalted water until soft – typically 45-75 minutes. Drain and leave to go cold. You can freeze them at this point, if you want to make some extra for another time. Rinse canned peas carefully before you use them. In the United States, avoid sugared garbanzos!

•

Peel the garlic and chop it finely in a food processor. Add the chickpeas (garbanzo beans) and chop. Add the oil and lemon juice slowly and alternately. You may have to take the lid off the food processor a couple of times to push the mixture back down. Some people like it really oily, and others don't; experiment to see what proportions suit you best. In any case, the hummus should be reasonably stiff, not a sloppy paste like most store-bought varieties. Season to taste with salt. Garnish with pitted black olives.

•

There will be slight differences in both texture and flavour between hummus made using canned beans and hummus made with soaked and boiled beans. If you can spare the time, the soaked and boiled beans are better. And, of course, the extra virgin oil makes all the difference compared with the nasty vegetable oils used by commercial manufacturers.

Some people add 30-100g/1-4 oz of tahini to the mixture; others (including us) actively dislike its taste.

TZATZIKI

300ml/1/2 pt/1 1/4 cups Greek yoghurt
1/2 cucumber (a piece about 15cm/6 in long)
Handful of fresh mint leaves

Thick, full-cream Greek style strained yoghurt is incomparably better for this dish than low-fat yoghurt. If you cannot get Greek, at least use full-cream yoghurt.

•

Partially peel the cucumber, alternating peeled and unpeeled strips. Unpeeled may have too much tough skin; fully peeled won't have the proper texture or colour. Chop finely, but don't put it through a processor. Drain it if it is too wet, Chop the mint leaves finely, saving a couple of sprigs for garnish: you should end up with 30-45ml/2-3 tbsp of chopped mint. Mix the yoghurt, cucumber and mint together. That's all there is to it.

MEXICAN DIPS

Corn chips or tostaditas *on their own are pretty dull, especially the commercial variety. Served with traditional Mexican salsa and guacamole, it is a very different story. Normally, both tomato salsas described below are served at the same time. The recipe for making* tostaditas *from scratch is on page 73.*

Salsa Fresca (Salsa Cruda)

350g/12 oz fresh tomatoes or 1 medium can
1 small red onion, or 2 shallots
1-4 cloves garlic

1-3 fresh hot green chilli peppers
fresh coriander leaves to taste

If you are using fresh tomatoes, peel and chop. Remove the seeds from the peppers. Finely chop all the ingredients together: the coriander "to taste" can be anything from 5ml/1 tsp to a handful (we incline towards the handful). If you grow your own coriander, and can get fresh green coriander seeds, crush a few of these and add them to the sauce. Some people add small quantities, maybe 15ml/1 tbsp each, of red wine vinegar or olive oil or both.

•

This *salsa* can be used immediately, but may be left in the refrigerator overnight. It may even improve with keeping; it will certainly get hotter.

Cooked Tomato Salsa

1 large clove garlic
1 shallot or small onion
15ml/1 tbsp olive oil
1 x 400g/14 oz can
   chopped tomatoes

1.5-2.5ml/1/4–1/2 tsp chilli powder
1.5ml/1/4 tsp chopped fresh or dried oregano
1.5ml/1/4 tsp dried thyme
1.5ml/1/4 ground cumin

Peel and finely chop the garlic and shallot or onion. Over a gentle heat, fry these in oil in a heavy pan until they are reduced to a purée. Turn up the heat. Add the tomatoes and other ingredients and bring to the boil. Simmer for 5-10 minutes, stirring from time to time: the objective is to break down the tomatoes and marry all the flavours. Sieve to give a smooth purée. If it is too liquid, return the purée to the pan and reduce over a moderate heat, stirring constantly. Serve hot or cold.

Guacamole

1-2 dried red chilli peppers
15ml/1tbsp boiling water
1 clove garlic (optional)

6 small or 4 large avocados
juice of 1/4 lemon (optional)

In a large pestle and mortar, finely pound the dried peppers. Add a tablespoon or so of boiling water and pound again. Then add the garlic clove and crush that thoroughly.

•

Peel and seed the avocados, and crush them with the pepper and garlic paste, taking care to mix well.

•

If you are not serving the guacamole immediately, squeeze the juice of a quarter of a lemon over the top to stop it going brown.

POTATO SALADS

Cold potato salads are probably most popular in the two countries that were for most of the twentieth century deadly enemies. In Russia they are an all but essential part of zakuski, *and in the United States they are almost a patriotic duty on the Fourth of July. The Russian versions are generally less cloying.*

POTATO AND EGG SALAD

4 large cold boiled potatoes (about 500g/1 lb)
4 hard-boiled eggs
120ml/4 fl oz/1/2 cup mayonnaise (page 115)
1 stick celery (optional)
2.5ml/1/2 tsp finely chopped fresh parsley
2.5ml/1/2 tsp finely chopped fresh oregano (optional)
2.5ml/1/2 tsp finely chopped fresh thyme (optional)
salt and pepper

Cut the potatoes into dice, up to about 2cm/3/4 in each side. Quarter the eggs, then cut each quarter in half again. Cut the celery into small dice, if using.

•

Mix all the ingredients, and season with salt and pepper. The oregano and thyme lift the salad from being merely pleasant to being quite remarkable.

POTATO AND BEET SALAD

4 large cold boiled potatoes (about 500g/1 lb)
2 large cold boiled beetroot (red beets)
120ml/4 fl oz/1/2 cup mayonnaise (page 115)
5ml/1 tsp finely chopped fresh basil (optional)
salt and pepper

Dice the potatoes and beetroot into 2cm (3/4 in) dice. Mix all the ingredients together – the basil is optional but highly desirable. The earthiness of the beetroot contrasts well with the flavour and texture of the potatoes.

POTATO AND TUNA SALAD

4 large cold boiled potatoes (about 500g/1 lb)
2 x 200g/7 oz cans tuna in oil
4-6 spring onions (scallions)
120ml/4 fl oz/1/2 cup mayonnaise (page 115)

Dice the potatoes into 2cm (3/4 in) dice. Drain the tuna, and flake it into pieces. Chop the spring onions (scallions), green parts and all. Mix everything together with the mayonnaise. This recipe was very popular in the United States Marine Corps, so it is ideal for the Fourth of July!

VARIATIONS

As with pasta salads (page 47), there are innumerable variations on potato salads. Instead of mayonnaise, you can use heavily seasoned soured (dairy sour) cream, yoghurt, *crème fraîche*, etc. – this is quite common in Russia – and you can try all kinds of ingredients. One mixture which we like, which is totally non-traditional, is potatoes mixed with feta in oil (page 118). The oil with its thyme and peppers are the only dressing you need. Another good mixture is baby boiled new potatoes in dill sauce (page 23).

•

It is important to keep the dressing in any potato salad to a minimum, or the salad rapidly becomes cloying. This is especially true if you use a proprietary mayonnaise. A rather oily home-made mayonnaise is best; if you do not make your own mayonnaise, then mix a good proprietary mayonnaise with a little extra virgin olive oil and some double (heavy) cream.

•

Rather than making a full recipe of one kind of potato salad, consider making half-recipes of two kinds: the extra effort is negligible, and it tastes (and looks) more interesting.

EGGS EN COCOTTE

Strictly speaking, eggs en cocotte *(in buttered ramekins) may be cooked with no additional ingredients, but they are greatly improved by adding cheese and* crème fraîche.

INGREDIENTS

100g/4 oz cheese (preferably Gruyère)
4 eggs
250ml/8 fl oz/1 cup *crème fraîche*
15ml/1 tbsp melted butter

Preheat the oven to about 225°C/425°F/Mark 7. Fill a baking dish or roasting pan about 2cm/3/4 in deep with water and place in the oven to warm.

•

Butter the interiors of the ramekins. Grate (shred) the cheese finely. Divide just over half the cheese between the four ramekins. Break an egg into each ramekin (carefully!). Spoon the *crème fraîche* over the eggs. Divide the remaining cheese between the four ramekins.

•

Place the ramekins in the baking dish in the oven, and bake. The French, who like their eggs barely cooked, would leave them as little as 10-12 minutes. We use about 15 minutes. If you like your eggs well done, you may leave them for 20 minutes or even longer, but the yolk will be hard and some of the textural appeal of the dish will be lost.

VARIATIONS

We have made eggs *en cocotte* using *fromage frais* or rich Greek-style yoghurt instead of *crème fraîche*, and you could probably use thick double (heavy) cream (including clotted cream), *crema Mexicana* or even soured (dairy sour) cream equally well. However you make it, this is a very rich dish. Serve with French bread or wholemeal crusty bread.

MUSHROOMS
STUFFED WITH SAUSAGE

A grilled or fried mushroom filled with fried chorizo or similar sausage is a classic Spanish tapa. You can, however, use almost any spicy sausage, including the Polish zywiecka, Spanish cabanos or even American "Italian sausage" – all of which keep well in the freezer and can be thawed rapidly.

INGREDIENTS

175ml/6 oz spiced sausages   50g/2 oz/1/4 cup butter
15ml/1 tbsp oil   4-12 open cup mushrooms, depending on size

Dice the sausages. Heat the oil in a small frying pan (skillet), and slowly render the diced sausages in their own fat. When they are well rendered, add the rendered fat to the butter in a larger frying pan, and fry the mushrooms. Divide the sausage between the mushrooms, and serve hot on hot plates. Crusty bread and red wine make an excellent accompaniment.

PRAWN COCKTAIL

Most people never have a properly made prawn cocktail, and therefore go through life imagining that they are not worth bothering with; but, like many other appetizers, a well-prepared version can be a revelation.

INGREDIENTS

3 shallots
120ml/4 fl oz/1/2 cup white wine
  or dry sherry
Chinese leaves (Nappa cabbage) or iceberg
  lettuce
15ml/1 tbsp mixed English (hot) mustard
15ml/1 tbsp finely chopped fresh tarragon

15-30ml/1-2 tbsp tomato purée (paste)
250ml/8 fl oz/1 cup mayonnaise (page 115)
60ml/4 tbsp cognac (optional)
salt, pepper and cayenne for seasoning
200-250g/7-8 oz cooked, peeled prawns
  (shrimps)

Chop the shallots finely. In a small, heavy-based saucepan, simmer them slowly in the wine until they are soft and the wine has reduced to nothing. Allow to cool.

•

Shred enough Chinese leaves (Nappa cabbage) to make a bed in each of four sundae glasses: five to ten leaves should be enough. Part of the attraction of a well-made prawn cocktail is the contrast between the crisp freshness of the bed and the richness of the top, so floppy lettuce is no good.

•

Mix the mustard, tarragon, cognac and tomato purée with the mayonnaise, which should be a little oilier then usual. Stir in the shallots. Season heavily, Dress the prawns or shrimps with this, and divide equally between the sundae glasses. Serve cool, but not chilled excessively.

VARIATIONS

A traditional garnish is sliced hard-boiled egg and tomato, and some people dress the lettuce with a vinaigrette (page 114). A very successful base, used in the Far Western Tavern in Guadalupe on California's central coast, is chopped celery hearts. You can also use fresh or canned crab in place of the prawns.

Chapter Three

SUBSTANTIAL COOKED DISHES

Nachos

VEGETABLES WITH SET EGGS

These Greek dishes are not quite omelettes, and they are certainly not scrambled eggs, though they bear some resemblance to both. They are, however, delicious, quick and vegetarian.

EGGS WITH COURGETTES (ZUCCHINI)

1kg/2 lb courgettes (zucchini)
60ml/4 tbsp olive oil
60ml/4 tbsp butter
5-10ml/1-2 tsp chopped fresh parsley or dill
salt to taste (up to 2.5ml/1/2 tsp)
black pepper to taste
2 tomatoes (optional)
8-12 eggs, beaten
60-90ml/4-6 tbsp finely grated cheese

Wash the courgettes (zucchini) – *kolokithakia* in Greek – and slice them about 1cm/1/2 in thick. Heat the oil and butter together (or use all oil or all butter) in a large, heavy frying-pan (skillet). Add the courgettes (zucchini), parsley or dill and seasonings. If you are using tomatoes, peel them and chop them finely, and add them at the same time. Once the mixture is frying nicely, turn it down, cover, and leave to cook for anything up to 30 minutes.

•

At the end of this time, pour the eggs over the courgettes; sprinkle the cheese over the top and cook, covered again, for a further 10-30 minutes until the eggs are set (it depends on how firm you like your eggs, and how you are cooking them). Do not stir, or the mixture will be all wrong, and do not cook over too high heat or the eggs will burn on the bottom of the pan.

•

Retsina is the traditional accompaniment, but you can drink just about any wine or beer with this dish. Guinness is good.

EGGS WITH TOMATOES

1 medium onion
120ml/4 fl oz/1/2 cup olive oil
750g/1 1/2 lb ripe tomatoes, peeled and sliced
salt to taste (up to 2.5ml/1/2 tsp)
black pepper to taste
5ml/1 tsp sugar (optional)
6-8 eggs

Finely chop the onion and fry in the oil until it is soft. Add all the other ingredients except the eggs; you will only need the sugar if the tomatoes are not sweet enough. Do not stir, or the tomatoes will break up. Simmer, covered, for 30 minutes. Then add the eggs, either beaten or broken individually on top of the mixture. Cook for a further 7-10 minutes, or to taste. If you break the eggs individually, use the lower number of eggs, and take care not to overcook the yolks.

GRISSINI

Grissini – bread sticks – are a fundamental accompaniment to Italian appetizers. The vast majority of mass-produced commercial grissini *are hardly worth eating, though, and the best of them only just approach the quality of home-made. The version below is typical of the Val d'Aosta, gnarly in shape and flavoured with olives and basil.*

INGREDIENTS

Yield: approximately 24 small *grissini*

1 sachet (6g/1/4 oz dried yeast)
5ml/1 tsp sugar
250ml/8 fl oz/1 cup warm water (blood heat)
30ml/2 tbsp olive oil
5ml/1 tsp salt
350g/12 oz/3 cups strong plain (all-purpose) flour
100g/4 oz olives
5ml/1 tbsp chopped fresh basil

Mix the yeast and sugar with the water; leave to stand for 5 minutes.

•

Mix the oil and salt with the flour. Make a well in the centre and add the water and yeast mixture. Mix and knead for 5-10 minutes, either in a large bowl or (if you have one) on a floured marble slab. Cover with oiled cling film and leave in a warm place to rise until it has roughly doubled in volume: this should take about 45 minutes.

•

Punch the dough down – you literally only need to hit it a couple of times – cover again and leave it to rest for 15 minutes. While it is resting, pit the olives and chop them. You can use black or green olives or a mixture of the two.

•

Work the olives and chopped basil into the dough. Cover again and let the dough rest for another 15 minutes or so. Take a piece of dough the size of a large walnut and roll with your fingers into a "snake" about 1-2cm/1/2 in in diameter. You do not need to allow any further rising time. Put the breadsticks on to a non-stick (or oiled) baking sheet. Bake in a preheated oven at about 180°C/350°F/Mark 4 for about 20 minutes or until they are dry, crisp and golden. They will keep for two or three days or longer in an airtight tin, and they can be refreshed with 5 minutes in a hot oven.

VARIATION

Omit the olives and basil, but roll the breadsticks in polenta before you cook them. You will need 50g/2 oz of polenta. Or roll the *grissini* in sesame seeds: again, you will need the same amount.

SPIEDINI

Preparing spiedini *is as much a matter of attitude as of following a recipe. You can put virtually anything on the skewers, and you can grill (broil), fry or barbecue them. Frying is easiest, and makes for the richest dish, but grilling (broiling) or barbecuing is better for you.*

PRAWN SPIEDINI

24-32 raw prawns (about 250g/8 oz)
100g/4 oz/1/2 cup butter
1 or more cloves garlic
8 bamboo skewers about 15cm/6 in long

Melt the butter in a small pan. Crush the garlic and add it. Soak the skewers for a few minutes in water: this will greatly reduce the risk of their burning. Thread the prawns onto the skewers: you should get three or four on to each skewer.

•

Brush the prawns with the garlic/butter mixture and grill (broil) or barbecue, brushing with additional butter and garlic from time to time, until they are pink and just cooked. Serve immediately, brushed with one last coat of butter and garlic.

MIXED SPIEDINI

100g/4 oz spicy sausage (*zywiecka*, *chorizo*, etc.)
200g/8 oz lean meat (pork, beef or lamb)
1 bell pepper (red, yellow or green)
2 small onions, about 5cm/2 in diameter
100g/4 oz large button mushrooms
350g/12 oz cherry tomatoes
12 bamboo skewers about 15cm/6 in long
oil for deep-frying

Cut the sausage, meat and pepper into convenient sizes for threading on the skewers. Quarter the onions. If you wash the mushrooms and tomatoes, dry them well. Do not soak the skewers!

•

Make up the skewers with a mixture of ingredients on each. You can even have the ingredients in bowls, and encourage your guests to make up their own mixtures: then they can make all-meat skewers, or all-vegetable skewers, if they wish. In this case you may find it desirable to double the quantities of everything, and make it a *spiedini* party.

•

Deep fry the *spiedini* in batches of about four. They will take anything from 1-2 minutes, depending on what ingredients you use and how well cooked you like your food.

•

Serve hot. Bread (especially Italian ciabatta bread) or *grissini* (bread sticks) and red wine are the ideal accompaniment – or you may prefer beer.

VARIATIONS

Other things you can put on the skewers include prawns, courgettes (zucchini),
lobster meat, smoked pork loin, Halloumi cheese, pieces of celery and cubes of
chicken breast.

•

If you grill (broil) or barbecue the mixed *spiedini* instead of deep-frying them,
make up a marinade as follows.

MARINADE

120ml/4 fl oz/1/2 cup olive oil
60ml/4 tbsp dry white wine
juice of 1/2 lemon
15ml/1 tbsp chopped fresh thyme or 5 ml/1 tsp dried

The proportions of wine to oil (1:2) are all that is important. You can vary the herbs
according to what you are cooking: rosemary is good on lamb, for example. Soak
the skewers before you use them, and marinate the prepared skewers for a few
minutes before cooking. During cooking, brush with the marinade.

CROSTINI

Crostini *are like a more elaborate version of* bruschetta *(page 20). Bread is toasted or dried in the oven, then topped with all kinds of things; the variety is limited only by your imagination. The example given here is typically Sicilian. We have allowed two slices each, but if people have less hearty appetites, there will be enough for more people.*

INGREDIENTS

700g/1 1/2 lb ripe tomatoes
4 cloves garlic
small handful of basil
60ml/4 tbsp olive oil
salt and pepper
1 small loaf of crusty, chewy bread
3-5 anchovy fillets
100-175g/4-6 oz Italian or Greek black olives

Skin the tomatoes (pour boiling water over them first), remove the cores and squeeze out the seeds. Chop the flesh coarsely. Peel and finely chop the garlic. Finely chop the basil, saving a few sprigs for garnish. Mix the tomato, garlic, basil and oil well, season, and leave in a bowl for at least 30 minutes and preferably 1 hour at room temperature for the flavours to marry.

•

Cut 8 slices from the loaf, each about 1cm/1/2 in thick. Toast in a preheated oven at 200ºC/400ºF/Mark 6 for about 10 minutes, turning once. The bread should be lightly browned. Use the bread hot, or let it cool to room temperature.

•

Chop the anchovies finely, and pit and chop the olives. Add them to the rest of the topping and mix in. Spoon this on to the bread, and spread it a little with the back of the spoon. Serve immediately: *crostini* becomes soggy after a few minutes. Plenty of robust red wine goes well with this dish.

SCALLOPS IN CHEESE AND SHERRY SAUCE

This is a variant on the French dish coquilles St Jacques Mornay. We borrowed it from Len, the landlord of our local pub the Bell, in St Nicholas at Wade, in Kent.

INGREDIENTS

8 large ("Queen") scallops
(about 750g/1 1/2 lb shelled)
100g/4 oz Gruyère cheese
50g/2 oz butter

50g/2 oz plain (all-purpose) flour
600ml/1 pt/1 1/4 US pts milk
60ml/4 tbsp sherry

Let the scallops come up to room temperature. Grate the cheese finely; if you cannot get Gruyère, other strong, hard cheeses will do. In a small pan, mix the butter and the flour, and heat gently until they begin to froth together. Stir well. Set this *roux* aside to cool.

•

Bring the milk almost to the boil. When it is quivering, put in the scallops. Simmer for 1-2 minutes. Remove the scallops with a slotted spoon, and set aside.

•

Add the cool roux to the hot milk, and stir in well; this is the opposite to the common procedure, when a cold liquid is added to a hot roux. It reduces the likelihood of lumps, and saves a great deal of time. When the sauce begins to thicken after a few minutes, add the grated cheese. Continue to stir, and add the sherry.

•

When you are confident that the sauce is as thick as it is going to get (it should be quite creamy), return the scallops to it for another minute or so, to allow them to heat through, and serve. We normally have some crusty French bread handy to mop up the extra sauce (there is plenty).

RATATOUILLE

Ratatouille is known by various names all around the Mediterranean, but it is essentially a variety of vegetables fried in richly flavoured olive oil, then stewed together.

INGREDIENTS

1 large aubergine (eggplant) (about 500g/1 lb)
5-10ml/1-2 tsp salt
500g/1 lb courgettes (zucchini)
500g/1 lb sweet bell peppers
500g/1 lb tomatoes, peeled, or 1 x 400g/14 oz can tomatoes
2 large onions
1 clove to 1 head garlic
120-180ml/4-6 fl oz/1/2–3/4 cup olive oil
30ml/2 tbsp chopped fresh basil (optional)

The proportions and precise quantities are not critical, and of course you can use several small aubergines (eggplants) instead of one large one. Also, the amount of oil you use is a matter of personal taste: we would use the larger amount, but some people might find the end result too oily. The same goes for the garlic: a whole head is not too much for some people.

•

Do not peel the aubergine (eggplant). Slice it into pieces 1-2cm/1/2–3/4 in thick. Sprinkle the slices with salt and leave them to purge for 20 minutes or more. Slice the courgettes (zucchini) into pieces up to 2.5cm/1 in thick. Core the peppers to remove the seeds, and cut into rings or slices or chunks. Halve or quarter the tomatoes: you can leave them unpeeled, or you can peel them first (pour boiling water over them to loosen the skins). Peel the onion and slice it into rings. Peel and chop or crush the garlic.

•

Heat about one quarter of the oil (30-45ml/2-3 tbsp) in a heavy frying pan (skillet). Over a gentle heat, fry the onions and the garlic for 5-10 minutes until the onions are soft. Transfer them to a large, heavy pan with a lid.

•

Next, in 60-90ml/4-6 tbsp of oil, fry the aubergine (eggplant) until soft. Transfer to the large pan.

•

In the remaining oil, fry the courgettes (zucchini), then the peppers, and finally the tomatoes. If you are using canned tomatoes, there is no need to fry them. Transfer to the large pan. Mix everything well, season and add the basil. Reduce the heat and simmer for at least 20 minutes and at most about 1 hour, depending on how soft you want the vegetables. Serve with bread, especially Italian *ciabatta* bread, or *bruschetta* (page 20), and red wine.

VARIATION

After serving the ratatouille into individual bowls, put a slice of cheese on top of each serving – Mozzarella or Monterey Jack or even Cheddar – and encourage the cheese to melt with a few minutes in a hot oven or under the grill (broiler) or even a microwave.

TORTILLAS

The tortilla, a flat pancake of unleavened bread made from flour or cornmeal, is basic to Mexican and Central American cuisine. Tortillas are used in a number of appetizers in this book. If you cannot buy them, they are easy to make and home-made taste even better.

CORN TORTILLAS

250g/8 oz/2 cups *masa harina*
250–375ml/8-13 fl oz/1–1 1/2 cups water

2.5ml/1/2 tsp salt

Measuring volumes, rather than weight, is the quickest and easiest way to make tortillas. The precise size of the cup does not matter, as long as you use the same cup for both measures. Using a standard American cup (250ml/8 fl oz) makes about 18 10cm/4 in tortillas – about enough for four people. You can freeze leftover tortillas.

•

Mix one cup of water with the *masa harina* (a fine-ground cornmeal, treated with lime) and the salt. This will probably result in too dry a dough, so go on adding water until the dough is just short of sticking to your fingers; 11/2 cups is the maximum you will need, depending on the freshness of the *masa harina*. If you add too much water, add a little more *masa harina*. You cannot overwork this dough: the more you handle it, the better it seems to get.

•

Take a piece of dough the size of a medium to large walnut and roll it into a ball between your hands. Place it between two plastic bags, and either with a tortilla press or a rolling pin, roll it out to a circle 10-15cm/4-6 in in diameter.

•

Without using any oil, heat a heavy frying pan (skillet), or a griddle, or a Central American *comal* and cook first one side of each tortilla and then the other. Press them down with a spatula: they should puff up when they are almost cooked. Cook until they begin to brown in spots; they should be a uniform golden colour elsewhere. Stack with a napkin around them to keep them warm. You can reheat them in a microwave, but they are better served within a few minutes of cooking.

WHEAT FLOUR TORTILLAS

250g/8 oz/2 cups plain white (all-purpose) flour
5ml/1 tsp salt
30ml/2 tbsp lard
about 250ml/8-10 fl oz/1 cup or more warm water
Flour for kneading and rolling

Sift the flour and salt together. Work the lard in with your fingers, then gradually add water to make a firm, non-sticky dough. Knead thoroughly, working in more flour if the dough is at all sticky.

•

Form the dough into balls: egg-sized for small (20cm/8 in) tortillas, the size of your fist for big ones (30-46cm/12-18 in). Press or roll as described above. Leave to stand for 20 minutes or more.

•

Heat a large griddle, *comal, tawa* or iron frying pan (skillet). Over a medium heat, cook the tortillas for 2 minutes on one side and 1 minute on the other; use no oil on the griddle. Serve immediately, or keep warm, or set aside for reheating or even freezing: flour *tortillas* are amazingly forgiving.

CARNE MOLIDA CRUDA

350-400g/12-14 oz first-class lean beef
juice of 1/2 lemon or 1 small lime
30ml/2 tbsp brandy (optional)
1-2 fresh, hot chilli peppers
1/2 small onion or 2-3 shallots
black pepper, cornichons and capers for garnish

This is a Central American version of *steak tartare*. Cut the beef into chunks about 2.5cm/1 in per side. Remove any gristle, membranes, etc.; you should end up with 300-350g/10-12 oz of meat. Marinate this in the lemon or lime juice and brandy, if using, for 5 minutes to 1 hour. The longer it marinates, the more tender the beef will be but the more pronounced the lemon flavour will be, too.

•

Chop the pepper(s) and onions or shallots finely. Remove the meat from the marinade, draining it somewhat, and chop it as for steak tartare. Do not chop too finely: there should still be a detectable texture, not a smooth brown paste. Mix the pepper and onion with the beef.

•

Divide the meat into four, and place on small 10cm/4 in tortillas. Season with pepper. Garnish with sliced cornichons and capers. Serve with red wine or Champagne.

QUESADILLAS

One of the great attractions of tortilla-based antojitos *or Mexican starters is that the tortillas themselves keep half-way to forever in the freezer and thaw in a few minutes – but once they are thawed, you can make food which is so traditional that the Great Incas themselves would recognise it.*

BASIC QUESADILLAS

4 large flour tortillas (about 25cm/10 in)
175g/6 oz cheese, preferably Monterey Jack, hard Mozzarella or Cheddar
a little butter

Grate or thinly slice the cheese.

•

Heat a large, heavy iron frying pan (skillet), or better still an old-fashioned griddle or a Central American *comal*. Use no oil or butter: the tortilla is "dry fried". When the pan is hot, place a tortilla on it and press it down with a spatula. Butter the upper side lightly.

•

After 1-2 minutes, when one side of the tortilla is thoroughly hot, flip it over with the spatula and, working quickly, put one quarter of the cheese in the middle. Fold the tortilla in half, over the cheese, and press down with the spatula. About 30 seconds later, turn the *quesadilla* over to brown the other side. The butter makes the outside wonderfully crisp, and the cheese melts on the inside. This is a very quick, easy *antojito*, and goes very well with a beer or a glass of red wine.

QUESADILLAS DE LUXE

In addition to the cheese, you can add a spoonful of refried beans (page 70); a little guacamole (page 51); and a small amount of shredded Chinese leaves (Nappa cabbage); a few slices of tomato; and some *crema Mexicana* or *crème fraîche*. You can even add shredded meat or *machomo* (page 70). Ideally, if you are making this sort of big, luxurious *quesadilla*, you should use the biggest size of tortilla you can get (30cm/12 in), and you will therefore need a large griddle.

QUESADILLAS SINCRONIZADAS

8 corn or flour tortillas, 10-15cm/4-6 in across
4 slices cheese, slightly smaller than the tortillas

Heat the pan, griddle or *comal* and place a tortilla on it. Put a slice of cheese on top, then another tortilla. Press down with a spatula. After 1-2 minutes, as the cheese begins to melt and the lower tortilla begins to brown, flip the *quesadilla* over to brown the other side and complete the melting of the cheese.

NACHOS

*Nachos are the Mexican appetizer par excellence, a combination of beans, cheese and corn chips.
They vary widely in elaborateness, but they are always served hot. Everyone shares the same plate,
picking out chips and scooping up the goodies. You can make them without the shredded meat
(below) and you can use canned beans; but like most things, they will taste better made from scratch.*

FRIJOLES (BEANS)

250g/8 oz dried red, kidney, pinto or lima (navy) beans, or one large can
1 medium onion
3-6 cloves garlic
1 bay leaf
1-2 Serrano chillies or 1 jalapeño pepper
30ml/2 tbsp lard or olive oil
5ml/1 tsp salt, or to taste
1 small tomato

Wash and pick over the beans: do not soak them. Finely chop the onion and garlic,
add half of them to the beans with the bay leaf and the chillies but not the salt.
Cover with cold water and bring to the boil. Boil for 10 minutes then simmer
gently. Add more water as necessary. When the beans begin to wrinkle, add 15ml/1
tbsp of lard or oil then continue cooking until the beans are soft. This can take all
day. When they are soft, add the salt and cook for another 30 minutes, without
adding any more water.

•

In the other tablespoon of oil or lard, gently cook the remaining onion and garlic
until they are golden. Skin, seed and chop the tomato then add it to the pan and
cook for another 2-3 minutes. Add 15-20ml/1-2 tbsp of the beans (in their cooking
liquid) and mash together. Use this mixture to thicken the beans in the beanpot.

FRIJOLES REFRITOS (REFRIED BEANS)

Beans, prepared as above
250g/8 oz/1 cup lard

Soften the lard to a spooning consistency. Melt about 30ml/2 tbsp of the lard in a
heavy frying pan (skillet). Mash 30ml/2 tbsp of cooked beans into this. Continue to
add the beans, about 15ml/ 1 tbsp at a time, mashing as you go. Add more lard
from time to time: the end result should be thick, fairly dry, and very rich and
creamy. You can reduce the amount of lard, though you will lose some of the
richness and creaminess, or you can substitute olive oil – not very traditional, but it
makes a great mixture.

•

To make a bean dip, use the same technique of making a pepper-and-garlic paste
as in *guacamole* (page 51): four dried chilli peppers and two cloves of garlic will
make a potent dip out of half the above recipe of *refritos*.

SHREDDED MEAT

1kg/2 lb boneless beef or pork or chicken
1-2 dried hot red chillies
1 small onion
5ml/1 tsp black peppercorns
5-20ml/1-2 tsp salt
1 bay leaf

Leave the meat in one piece. Choose the smallest pan that will accommodate it, and cover it with water: the smaller the volume of water proportional to the volume of meat, the better the end result will taste. Tear or shred the chillies finely and add them to the pan with the other ingredients. Bring to the boil and simmer for 2-3 hours; the meat should be so tender it is falling apart. Check periodically to make sure the meat is still covered. If it is not, then add more water. Leave the meat to cool in the cooking liquid.

•

Take the meat out of the broth or jelly (it may have set as it cools), and tease it into shreds with two forks. Use it in whatever recipes call for it.

•

The cooking liquid can be strained to make an excellent stock for Chinese soups, or anywhere else you need stock.

•

If you make shredded beef, you can further cook it to make *machomo*: melt 50g/2 oz/ 1/4 cup of lard in a heavy pan, and add the shredded beef. Fry at a moderate to high heat, stirring constantly, until the beef is dark brown and crispy. This is used as a garnish: as a filling for tacos; and as an accompaniment to *huevos rancheros* (page 94).

NACHOS

250g/8 oz beans or 1 small can refried beans
500g/1 lb *tostaditas* or corn chips (page 73)
250g/8 oz shredded meat (beef or chicken)
100g/4 oz/1 cup finely grated cheese
50g/2 oz black olives, pitted and sliced
2-4 fresh or preserved jalapeño peppers
60-120ml/2-4 fl oz/1/4–1/2 cup *crema Mexicana, crème fraîche* or soured (dairy sour) cream
50-100g/2-4 oz/1/4–1/2 cup *guacamole* (page 51) (optional)

Heat the beans and make a mound in the middle of a plate. This is the foundation of the *nachos*. Stick the corn chips into the beans, with the shredded meat scattered in and around the corn chips. If you make your *tostaditas* yourself, they are stronger then the commercial corn chips and easier to embed; with commercial chips, you just scatter them.

•

Scatter the grated cheese on top of this. If the *nachos* are made properly, with freshly fried, hot *tostaditas* , the cheese will melt of its own accord. Otherwise, 2-5 minutes in a preheated oven at 220°C/425°F/Mark 7 will melt the cheese.

•

Now add the olives, and then the peppers, sliced into rings. Remove the seeds if you are using fresh peppers! Finally, put a dollop of *crema Mexicana,, crème fraîche* or soured (dairy sour) cream on top, along with a little *guacamole* if you have some; serve cooked and raw *salsas* (page 51) on the side. After 1-2 hours, *nachos* become leathery and unattractive, so serve them as soon as possible after assembly.

TOSTADITAS,
TOSTADAS AND TACOS

A tostadita *is a proper, made-from-scratch corn chip, as used with Mexican dips (page 51) or in* nachos *(page 70). A* tostada *is a fried tortilla with garnish, and a* taco *is just a tortilla (page 66) wrapped in a U-shape around a filling.*

TOSTADITAS

corn tortillas (page 66)
oil or lard for deep-frying

Either use very small ready-cooked tortillas, at most 5cm/2 in in diameter, or cut larger cooked tortillas into quarters. Deep-fry for 5-7 minutes; some people like them light golden, others deep brown.

TOSTADAS

4 small (10-15cm/4-6 in) corn tortillas (page 66)
100-175g/4-6 oz Chinese leaves (Nappa cabbage)
2 medium-sized tomatoes
100g/4 oz/1/2 cup refried beans (page 70) or use canned
250g/8 oz shredded meat or chicken (page 70) (optional)
120ml/4 fl oz/1/2 cup soured (dairy sour) cream or *crema Mexicana*
50g/2 oz cheese, grated
oil for frying

Fry and drain the tortillas. Shred the Chinese leaves (Nappa cabbage). Chop the tomatoes coarsely. Divide the ingredients between the tortillas. The Chinese leaves (Nappa cabbage) go on first: then the beans; then the meat; then the tomatoes, cheese and *crema Mexicana.*

•

A *tostada grande* is normally made with a large wheat flour tortilla, up to 40cm/16 in across. It is again deep-fried, then shaped into a bowl, but there is more filling and it is more lavish: often *guacamole* and *salsa cruda* (*salsa fresca* – both page 51) are also added. You will need to double the above quantities at least, in order to fill a *tostada grande.*

TACOS

8 corn tortillas, 15cm/6 in in diameter (page 66)
250-500g/8 oz – 1 lb *carnitas* or shredded meat

A taco is the simplest form of stuffed Mexican pancake. A soft taco is a fresh tortilla loosely wrapped around some sort of filling, most usually shredded meat, while a crisp or fried taco is the same thing, using a tortilla that has been deep-fried and moulded into a U-shape. Soft tacos are served hot, and not garnished; fried tacos may be served hot or cold, often garnished with tomato and lettuce or Chinese leaves (Nappa cabbage). Beer is the normal drink with tacos. It does not need to be Mexican beer; almost any beer is good, including Guinness.

SAUSAGE AND BEANS

*This is rather different from the cowboy fare suggested by the name; the richness of the grilled
sausage contrasts well with the blandness of the beans.*

INGREDIENTS
500g/1 lb *zywiecka, cabanos* or similar spiced sausage
350g/12 oz boiled or canned butter beans
Parsley to garnish

For thin sausages such as *cabanos*, cook the sausage whole or in manageable lengths
(10-15cm/4-6 in). For thick sausages, cut the whole sausages into manageable
lengths and split them almost all the way through. Open them out to give a
"B" shape.

•

Grill (broil) under a moderate heat, or better still barbecue, giving the fat plenty of
time to render out. Warm the beans; serve the sausage hot or warm, with the beans,
garnished with basil or parsley.

FALAFEL

Falafel – fried chickpea (garbanzo beans) balls or croquettes – are found all over the Near and Middle East. They can be eaten on their own, or they can be used to fill a pitta sandwich. They can be rather dry unless served with an accompanying sauce.

INGREDIENTS

225g/8 oz dried chickpeas (garbanzo beans) or 1 350g/12 oz can
1-2 cloves garlic (optional)
2 eggs
100g/4 oz/1/2 cup dried breadcrumbs
30ml/2 tbsp olive oil
2.5ml/1/2 tsp salt
1-1.5ml/1/8–1/4 tsp ground cumin
1.5-2.5ml/1/4–1/2 tsp Tabasco or similar hot pepper sauce
oil for deep-frying

Soak dried chickpeas (garbanzo beans) for 8-12 hours then boil (without salt) until tender – about 45-90 minutes. You should end up with about 350g/12 oz of cooked, drained chickpeas (garbanzo beans), but the exact weight will depend on the freshness of the dried peas. You can freeze them once cooked. If you are using a can, drain and rinse carefully.

•

Using a food processor or a pestle and mortar, chop or mash the chickpeas (garbanzo beans) coarsely. Peel and crush the garlic, if using; add to the chickpeas (garbanzo beans), along with the eggs, oil, spices and seasonings. Add enough breadcrumbs (about 30ml/2 tbsp) to make a dough which can be moulded in the fingers. You can also freeze the mixture at this stage.

•

Form the mixture into patties, or into balls about 2.4cm/1 in in diameter. Roll these in breadcrumbs before deep frying (in batches) in hot oil at 180°C/360°F for 2-4 minutes or until golden brown. Serve hot. A hearty red wine makes an excellent accompaniment.

SAUCE

30ml/2 tbsp tahini
juice of 1 small lemon

1 clove garlic
15-30ml/1-2 tbsp water

Whisk the lemon juice into the tahini. It will thicken like glue. Peel and crush the garlic and add it; mix well. Add the water and whisk to the desired consistency – how much water you need will depend on your lemon and your tahini. Strain through a tea-strainer to remove any large lumps of garlic. Serve with the falafel.

VARIATIONS

The spicing can be varied widely according to taste: basil, marjoram, thyme and coriander (fresh or ground) are all possibilities, and you can even add chopped fresh chilli peppers. Instead of breadcrumbs, you can mix them with bulgar wheat.

•

An alternative sauce is simply thick Greek-style yoghurt with plenty of chopped fresh mint mixed in with it.

ALBONDIGUITAS

Albondiguitas *are the spiced meatballs also found in* albondigas *soup; they are served on their own, or with a tomato sauce all over Spain.*

INGREDIENTS

250g/8 oz lean minced (ground) beef
175g/6 oz minced (ground) pork
50g/2 oz/1/3 cup cooked long-grain rice
1 shallot or very small onion, very finely chopped
1-2 cloves garlic, very finely chopped
1 egg
5-15ml/1–3 tsp chopped fresh coriander (optional)
salt and pepper to taste
lard or oil for frying

Mix all the ingredients thoroughly. If you are using a food processor, begin with the onion, garlic and coriander, then add the rest. Form into balls the size of a walnut. In oil heated to 190°C/375°F, fry for about 6 minutes – it takes quite a long time for them to cook through.

•

Serve with cocktail sticks (toothpicks), or in a tomato sauce (page 87) or ranchera sauce (page 94).

SCOTCH EGGS

*Scotch eggs are pub food, probably the nearest the British intentionally come to tapas.
Shop-bought eggs can be all right, but home-made ones with sausage meat from a good local
butcher are enormously better. They also contain far fewer preservatives.*

INGREDIENTS

5-6 small eggs

250g/8 oz sausage meat

100g/4 oz/2/3 cup breadcrumbs

oil for deep-frying

Hard-boil 4 of the eggs. When they are cool enough to handle, peel them and cover them with as even a layer of sausage meat as you can manage. Try to keep it as thin as possible, about 5mm/1/4 in.

•

Beat the remaining egg(s), and dip the Scotch eggs first in the egg, and then the breadcrumbs. For a really crisp coating, beat 2 eggs and double-coat the Scotch eggs with egg and breadcrumbs.

•

Deep-fry the Scotch eggs immediately in very hot oil at 170º-190ºC/350º-375ºF for 6-8 minutes; you need to be sure that the sausage meat is thoroughly cooked. They are best eaten after they have cooled to around room temperature, but before the breadcrumbs have lost their crispiness. English mustard (preferably mixed with beer) and plenty of strong ale are ideal accompaniments.

SEEKH KEBAB

Kebabs in India are normally made of finely minced meat moulded into sausage shapes or patties, served on their own or with a little salad, rather than with bread.

INGREDIENTS

500ml/1 lb minced (ground) beef
1 large onion
1-2 green chilli peppers, seeded and finely chopped
1-2 cloves garlic
5ml/1 tsp garam masala
5ml/1 tsp tandoori masala

5ml/1 tsp salt
2.5ml/1 tsp cumin seeds
2.5ml/1 tsp hot red chilli powder
15ml/1 tbsp finely chopped fresh ginger
15ml/1 tbsp finely chopped fresh coriander

Mix everything thoroughly in a food processor. The meat should be considerably more finely chopped than usual, as this helps it to stick together. Shape the mixture into eight sausages up to 15cm/6 in long, around metal or bamboo skewers. You can freeze them at this point.

•

Grill (broil) for 5-10 minutes, depending on the shape of the kebab and the heat of the grill (broiler); or shallow fry for 4-6 minutes; or deep-fry for 3-5 minutes; or barbecue for 5-8 minutes, turning occasionally. Barbecuing tastes best, but use a spatula to separate the kebabs from the grill – they will stick.

•

Serve hot, with beer or fresh lime soda (fizzy water and lime juice or lemon juice). Cooked kebabs can be reheated under the grill, or in the oven, or even the microwave, but they will not be as good.

VARIATIONS

You can use mutton or goat – Hindus do, if they eat meat at all – and you can vary the spicing infinitely to suit your personal taste. Some omit the green chillies, the ginger or the coriander, or all three; others add dried poppy seeds, or green mango powder, or different masalas or even hot (Madras) curry powder.

FRIED POTATO SKINS

This seems to be an authentically American appetizer; at least, we have never encountered it anywhere else. At its best, it is a superb blend of textures, flavours and temperatures, but all too often you will find that restaurant versions are lukewarm and soggy from being kept and reheated. Potato skins need to be assembled and served immediately.

INGREDIENTS

4 potatoes (2 halves per person)
6 rashers bacon
100g/4 oz cheese for grating
chives or spring onions (scallions)
100g/4 oz/1/2 cup soured (dairy sour) cream
oil for deep-frying

Choose a firm variety of potato which will not crumble when cooked. Scrub but do not peel the potatoes. Ideally, bake them in the oven; alternatively, cook them in the microwave or even boil them. They should be fully cooked.

•

Cook the bacon until it is crisp. A microwave is an easy way to do this, with the bacon resting on paper towels – our microwave takes 6 minutes, and we change the paper towels half way through. Crumble the crispy bacon into pieces. Grate the cheese: Cheddar or Monterey Jack is ideal. Chop the chives or spring onions (scallions).

•

Let the potatoes cool. Halve them, and scoop out the flesh to leave a wall up to 5mm/1/4 in thick. The thinner you can make the walls, the crispier the skins will be; this is why boiled potatoes are harder to handle than baked, and why cold potatoes are easier to handle than hot.

•

Heat the oil to 190ºC/375ºF (hot!) – and deep-fry the skins, turning them occasionally to make sure they are crisp and browned all over. Cook to taste: we like ours quite a deep brown. Remove with a slotted spoon and drain carefully. Arrange the skins on individual plates.

•

While the potatoes are still hot, add the grated cheese, leaving it for 1/2 minute to melt. Restaurants sometimes grill the skins at this stage to help the cheese melt, but this tends to soften the skins. Next add the soured (dairy sour) cream, and finally sprinkle bacon bits and chives over the top. Serve immediately: the dish remains good for up to 1 hour, but it is at its best when served within a couple of minutes of cooking.

VARIATIONS

You can put almost anything in the potato skins: for example, cottage cheese or cream cheese, with or without prawns or smoked salmon trimmings. Or you can try "ethnic" fillings such as taramasalata or tzatziki (pages 48) or *salsa fresca* (page 51). You can also mix the flesh of the potato with the soured (dairy sour) cream, cheese and chives, and put it back in the fried skin: this makes for a very substantial appetizer indeed. If you do this, it is a good idea to heat the stuffing under the grill (broiler) or in the microwave *before* you add it to the skins, to keep them crisp.

HOT PEPPERS STUFFED WITH CREAM CHEESE

Small hot peppers, even the notorious jalapeños, are tamed by stuffing them with cream cheese and deep-frying them in breadcrumbs. Even so, this remains a dish for those who love seriously hot food. If you do, it is unforgettable.

INGREDIENTS

24-32 small hot peppers, about 6cm/2 1/2 in long
175g/6 oz cream cheese
2 eggs
100g/4 oz/2/3 cup finely sifted breadcrumbs
50g/2 oz/1/2 cup plain (all-purpose) flour
oil for deep frying

Seed the peppers. This is the only part of this recipe which is at all difficult or time-consuming. The trick is to cut through the top, about two-thirds of the way around, so you cut through the central core of seeds. Then, make a slit down one side, from the centre of the first cut to the point of the chilli. The seeds should then come out in one piece, though you may have to scrape out a few more with the point of a knife. With practice, you can improve your speed from two peppers a minute to four or five peppers a minute.

•

Stuff the peppers with cream cheese, as full as they will go: if you squeeze a little out as you close them, just wipe it off. Do not worry about a little cheese on the skin: it will help the coating to stick.

•

Beat the eggs. Roll the peppers individually in flour, then in the beaten egg, then in the breadcrumbs. When you have coated them all once, coat them all a second time in egg then breadcrumbs.

•

Deep-fry them in hot-oil 350-375ºC/180-190ºF for about 4-5 minutes until they are a rich golden brown. Do not leave them in too long, or the cheese will begin to escape.

•

Drain on paper towels for a couple of minutes – this also allows them to fall to a temperature where the cheese will not burn your mouth – and serve hot. They remain good for half an hour or so. Mexican beer goes well with them; so does strong red wine. Normally, you would also have tortilla chips (*tostaditas*, page 73) and *salsa* (page 51 again) on the table. Blue corn chips go particularly well with this dish: they have a very slightly different aroma from yellow corn chips.

VARIATION

Instead of using an egg-and-breadcrumb coating, you can also coat these in the same sort of beaten egg that you would use for normal-sized *chilies rellenos* (page 88).

GARLIC SHRIMP

The very best gambas al ajillo *are made as in Spain with tiny shrimps, caught that day, but these are incredibly fiddly and time-consuming to prepare, so we use large fresh shrimps or prawns. We admittedly keep frozen prawns in the freezer, but only for emergencies. Either way, always start with the shrimps at room temperature: they will not cook properly from frozen, or even refrigerator temperature.*

GARLIC SHRIMP WITH OLIVE OIL

4 cloves garlic
1 dried red hot chilli
120ml/4 fl oz/1/2 cup olive oil
350g/12 oz shrimp or prawn tails, shelled

2.5ml/1/2 tsp paprika
15ml/1 tbsp finely chopped fresh parsley
salt

Peel and thinly slice the garlic; de-seed the hot chilli and tear it into 3-4 pieces. Over a fairly modest heat, heat the oil in a heavy pan or earthenware pot, with the garlic and chilli. As soon as the garlic turns golden, increase the heat somewhat and add the shrimp or prawns. Stirring rapidly, cook for 1 1/2–2 1/2 minutes. Do not overcook! Add the paprika and parsley, and salt to taste. Serve piping hot, with crusty bread to mop up the juice, and dry white wine or sherry.

GARLIC SHRIMP WITH BUTTER

4 cloves garlic
100g/4 oz/1/2 cup butter
350g/12 oz shrimp or prawn tails, shelled

60ml/4 tbsp dry or medium sherry
salt and pepper

Peel the garlic, and slice it thinly or crush it. Melt the butter in a heavy pan, and over a low heat, infuse the garlic into the butter. Over a slightly greater heat, cook the shrimps or prawns, stirring constantly, until they begin to look cooked. This takes less than 1 minute. Remove the shrimps from the butter; add the sherry, salt and pepper, and reduce over a fierce heat, stirring constantly. After a couple of minutes, return the shrimps or prawns to the pan to reheat for another 1/2 minute or so. Serve as above.

Chapter Four

CHALLENGING DISHES

Pâté of Smoked and Fresh Salmon

SASHIMI AND SUSHI

Sashimi *is normally made with raw fish;* sushi *can be made either with raw fish or with cooked fish; they tend to be something that most people either love or hate.*

THE FISH

500-750g/1-1 1/2 lb raw and/or cooked fish
Wasabi (Japanese horseradish)
Pickled ginger

If you use raw fish, it should be extremely fresh, or it should have been frozen when it was caught: most *sushi* bars use the latter sort.

•

Meticulously trim away all skin, gristle etc., so that all that is left is flawless flesh. Cut this, always on the bias, into bite-sized pieces: traditionally about 5-8cm/2-3 in long by 1-2cm/1/2–3/4 in thick by about 2.5cm/1 in wide. Served without rice, this is *sashimi*. Served with rice it becomes *sushi*.

•

The choicest raw fish are yellowtail (*buri* or *hamachi*), tuna (*maguro* or *otoro*), halibut (*hirame*) and sea bream (*tai*), served without further treatment. Salmon is today served the same way.

•

Prawns (*ebi*), squid (*ika*), abalone (*awabi*) and various clams were traditionally lightly boiled, but may also be served raw.

•

Fillets of mackerel (*saba*) and gizzard shad (*kohada*) are salted for a few hours, then marinated in sweetened vinegar for anything from 15 minutes upwards. They are served with the skin on.

•

Sea eel (*anago*) is braised, skin side down, in a boiling mixture of equal quantities of soy sauce, *saké, mirin* (cooking *saké*) and soy sauce for 7-8 minutes, then grilled (broiled) just before serving.

THE RICE

250g/8 oz short-grain Japanese-style rice
75ml/5 tbsp rice vinegar
75ml/5 tbsp sugar
salt to taste
wasabi (Japanese horseradish)

Wash the rice repeatedly, then soak it for 1 hour. In a pot with a tight-fitting lid, with just enough water to cover the rice, boil over a high heat for 2 minutes; a medium flame for 5 minutes; then a low flame for about 15 minutes to absorb the water. You can hear the cooking process: the rice bubbles at first, and then hisses when all the water is absorbed.

•

Make *sushi-zu* (sweetened vinegar) from equal volumes of rice vinegar and sugar. Heat the vinegar to dissolve the sugar, then cool rapidly. Salt heavily.

•

In a large non-metallic bowl, separate the grains of cooked rice with a wooden spoon. At the same time, have an assistant fan the rice to cool it, and add a few tablespoons of *sushi-zu*. It is a matter of taste how much (or how little) you use.

Cover the rice with a damp cloth to prevent it drying out.

•

Mould the sticky rice into little plinths with your fingers. Put a dab of *wasabi* on the underside of a piece of fish, and drape it over the rice. *Nori* (seaweed in sheets, which should be briefly toasted before use) is sometimes use to "tie" the fish to the rice, or to build little "battleships" (*gunkan-maki*) to hold soft ingredients like *uni* (sea urchin), roe of various kinds, scallops (*hotategai*) or oysters (*kaki*).

SERVING AND EATING

Arrange the *sashimi* or *sushi* on individual plates or on a single large serving plate: a wooden model boat is the traditional Japanese platter for a grand meal. Garnish with pickled ginger and small cones of *wasabi*. Fresh *wasabi* is grated from a root, but you can also buy it prepared in tubes, or as a powder to mix with water. If you cannot buy pickled ginger, slice fresh ginger root very thinly and pickle in rice vinegar: it is usable (though hot) after a few hours, and mellows with keeping.

•

Each person has a very small shallow bowl into which they pour soy sauce, and add *wasabi* according to their personal inclination, mixing the two well. The *sashimi* or *sushi* are dipped into this mixture immediately before eating. *Sashimi* is normally eaten with chopsticks, *sushi* with the fingers. Serve quickly: after an hour or so, both can dry out and become unattractive.

•

Hot *saké* or green tea are proper accompaniments, though Japanese beer or Scotch (or Japanese) whisky would also be normal in Japan. Sherry is surprisingly good, too.

SPANAKOPITTES

Spanakopittes are spinach-filled pies made with filo (phyllo) dough. They are a classic Greek light dish, and can be eaten hot or cold. They are still quite good when they are two or three days old, though they are best on the first day.

INGREDIENTS

750g/1 1/2 lb spinach
5ml/1 tsp salt
1-2 eggs
4-5 spring onions (scallions)
120ml/4 fl oz/1/2 cup olive oil
250g/8 oz feta cheese

150g/8 oz filo dough
15ml/1 tbsp chopped fresh dill
15ml/1 tbsp chopped fresh parsley (optional)
pepper
butter or oil for greasing

If the spinach is fresh, wash it and chop it. Mix the salt in well, and leave it for 1 hour. With thawed frozen spinach, just add the salt. Either way, squeeze it well to remove excess moisture. Beat the egg(s). Clean and chop the spring onions (scallions); add the spinach, along with 30ml/2 tbsp of olive oil and the eggs. Crumble the cheese, and mix it in well. Mix in the herbs.

•

If you are using frozen filo, or if it has been in the refrigerator, give it plenty of time to come up to room temperature. Cover the pastry you are not actually using with a damp cloth while you are working, or it will dry out.

•

Butter or oil a bun (muffin) tin. Cut the dough into pieces about 10cm/4 in square, or to suit your cooking tin. Lay a cut sheet of filo over one of the depressions in the tin, and brush it with olive oil. Push it down so that it lines the depression in the tin. Lay another sheet on top, slightly rotated, and oil it. Repeat until you have a stack of 6 sheets of filo dough, one on top of the other, with the corners sticking out all around the edges like the petals of a flower.

•

Fill the depression generously with the spinach mixture; there is no need to allow for expansion. Fill the remaining depressions in the same way; you should end up with 10-12 *spanakopittes*. Bake in a preheated oven at 150ºC/300ºF/Mark 2 for 40-45 minutes or until golden brown. Leave for a few minutes to cool: they will be too flexible to handle otherwise. Gently lift them out, which is much easier than it looks as if it is going to be.

•

If you like retsina, these go superbly with it. Otherwise you can drink pretty much anything you like.

BRAGOLI (BEEF OLIVES)

Paupiettes in French, beef olives in English, this Maltese dish is just thin pieces of meat rolled up and cooked. You can cook them stuffed or unstuffed; both options are described below.

UNSTUFFED BRAGOLI

500g/1 lb good roasting beef, cut into 8 thin slices
oil for deep-frying

Flatten the slices of meat with a meat hammer or rolling pin; roll up tightly. Secure with two half cocktail sticks (toothpicks). Deep fry to taste: about 2 minutes will leave it rare in the middle, while 4-5 minutes will leave it crispy on the outside and well done inside. Serve on their own, two per person, or with tomato sauce (see below).

STUFFED BRAGOLI

meat as above	15ml/1 tbsp chopped fresh parsley
175g/6 oz minced (ground) beef	salt and pepper
1 rasher of bacon or slice of ham	2 large celery stalks (optional)
100g/4 oz/2/3 cup breadcrumbs	oil for frying
1 egg	tomato sauce (below)

Fry the minced beef and bacon or ham together. Add the breadcrumbs, egg, parsley and seasoning. Spread out the meat slices: flatten with a meat hammer if necessary. Put 30ml/2 tbsp of the stuffing in the middle of each slice. Roll up, and tie using a piece of "string" stripped from a celery stalk – or use cocktail sticks (toothpicks), which is easier. Deep fry for 3-5 minutes.

•

Simmer in the tomato sauce below, for 20-40 minutes. When it comes to serving the beef olives, you will have more sauce than you need. The traditional Maltese answer to this is to serve the excess sauce on spaghetti, as a separate course.

TOMATO SAUCE

1 large onion
5 cloves garlic
1 x 400g/14 oz can tomatoes, chopped
1 x 100g/4 oz can tomato purée (paste)
1 wine-glass red wine (optional)
1 bay leaf
pinch each of parsley, sage, rosemary, thyme, oregano
15-30ml/1-2 tbsp olive oil
sugar if necessary

Finely chop the onion and garlic and fry gently in the olive oil until soft and golden. Add all the other ingredients, bring to the boil and simmer for 5-10 minutes. Taste: if the tomatoes or wine were a bit sharp, you may need to add some sugar to balance the flavour.

CHILES RELLENOS

Chiles rellenos – stuffed chillies – mean something quite different in Mexico from what they mean in Spain, where they refer to peppers (bell peppers) stuffed with a rice mixture.

INGREDIENTS

8 long green or red chillies (10-15cm/4-6 in)
6 eggs
250g/8 oz firm white cheese (Monterey Jack or hard Mozzarella)
lard or oil for frying

Blister the chillies over an open flame or under the grill. The skin should be at least three-quarters blistered and blackened. As each is blistered, put it into a bag or a pot with a tight-fitting lid. After a few minutes resting, the chillies will be cool enough to handle and the skins should scrape off easily.

•

Slit the chillies open from just below the stem to the point, and remove the core and all the seeds, but leave the stem as a "handle". Cut the cheese into sticks up to 1cm/1/2 in square and a little shorter than the chillies: the cheese has to fit inside the chilli, and the chilli must close over it. Once they are stuffed, roll them in flour and leave them to rest in the refrigerator for at least 30 minutes, more if possible.

•

When you are ready to cook, heat the oil or lard: about 4cm/1 1/2 in in a large frying pan (skillet). Separate the eggs. Beat the whites until they hold stiff peaks. Beat the yolks separately. Carefully fold the yolks into the whites. You have to use this mixture QUICKLY, as it separates in less than 15 minutes.

•

Dip the stuffed chilli into the egg mixture, covering it completely: this can take a little practice. As each chilli is coated, fry it in the oil. Turn it once (this is tricky, too). As soon as it is golden brown all over (about 3-5 minutes), take it out and drain it on paper towels. Cooked chillies can be kept warm in a cool oven while you finish the batch, but the sooner they are served and eaten, the better they taste.

•

Serve with *tostaditas* (page 73), *salsa fresca* (page 51) and refried beans (page 70).

VARIATION

You can stuff the chillies with refried beans (page 70) instead of with cheese: this is what the poor eat when they cannot afford cheese. We have even tried stuffing them with the potato curry filling on page 98, for a really cross-cultural dish!

DOLMADES

Dolmades (dolmathakia in Greek) are surprisingly easy to make. Vine leaves are readily available from most good supermarkets and delicatessens, and the rest of the ingredients are very easy to find. Use the strongest-flavoured Greek olive oil that you can get, as this is part of the secret of the taste.

INGREDIENTS

1 packet or can of vine leaves, or 36 fresh leaves
250g/8 oz onions or shallots
150ml/5 fl oz/2/3 cup olive oil
100g/4 oz/1/2 cup long-grain rice
15ml/1 tbsp chopped fresh dill or parsley
10ml/2 tsp salt
pepper to taste – up to 1.5ml/1/4 tsp
juice of 1 lemon

If you are using fresh vine leaves, blanch them in boiling water for 2 minutes until they are soft. If you are using preserved leaves packed in brine, rinse them, and use less salt in the stuffing.

•

Chop the onions or shallots and fry them in 60ml/4 tbsp olive oil until they are soft – 5-10 minutes. Add the uncooked rice and cook for another 5 minutes. Add the dill, salt and pepper and 250ml/8 fl oz/1 cup of water, and simmer for another 5 minutes. Leave the mixture to cool.

•

Remove the stems from the leaves. With the leaf shiny side down, put a generous teaspoon of filling in the middle. Fold the sides over the filling, and roll the leaf up. Do not roll too tightly, as the rice will swell slightly during cooking. You should end up with 15-20 dolmades.

•

Line a large, shallow pan with the remaining leaves – they help to flavour the rice – and pack the dolmades close together in the pan. Sprinkle with lemon juice, pour over the remaining olive oil, and add hot water until the dolmades are half-submerged. Weigh them down with a plate, to discourage them from unrolling, and simmer for about 1 hour. Leave them to cool in the same pan. Drain and serve, preferably as part of a *mezé* (page 91). They will keep for two to three days in the refrigerator, so you can make then well in advance.

•

There is no need for a sauce, but they go well with yoghurt or with tzatziki and taramasalata (page 48). Two per person is a normal first helping, but they make a good foil to the masses of meat that normally accompany *mezé*, so most people will eat more.

VARIATIONS

The two most common flavouring elements are pine nuts or currants, or both. For the above recipe, add 15ml/1 tbsp of pine nuts or 30ml/2 tbsp currants (or both) to the onion/rice mixture at the same time as the seasonings.

•

You can also fry about 100g/4 oz of minced (ground) lamb with the onions, for a non-vegetarian version. If you do, then reduce the quantity of rice by about half, and use less water in the meat/onion/rice mixture. As usual, the proportions are not very critical: you can use more or less meat, as you feel inclined.

MEZÉ

A full Near Eastern mezé *or* mezedes *will begin with Greek dips from page 48, and will then include* dolmades *(page 89), possibly a bean salad (page 38), lots of barbecued meat, as described below, very likely some* kalamares *(page 104), and quite likely a few other dishes as well.*

BARBECUED MEZÉ

100g/4 oz/1/2 cup butter
4 cloves garlic
150ml/5 fl oz/2/3 cup olive oil
juice of 1 lemon
30ml/2 tbsp chopped fresh mint
5ml/1 tsp dried or 15ml/1 tbsp chopped fresh thyme
8 small lamb cutlets
250g/8 oz Halloumi cheese
4 slices smoked pork loin
500g/1 lb boneless pork (leg or shoulder)
4 small fillet steaks (optional)
pitta bread

Fire up the barbecue. While it is getting warm, melt the butter in a small saucepan and crush the garlic into it. This is for basting the beef and the pork. In a shallow dish, mix the olive oil, lemon juice, mint and thyme. This is for marinating the lamb and for basting the lamb and the pork. Place the lamb cutlets in the mixture to marinate for a few minutes. Slice the Halloumi about 1cm/1/2 in thick. Slice the smoked pork loin to the same thickness. Cut the fresh pork into cubes 2cm/3/4 in on a side, and thread on to four skewers.

•

Before you put anything on the barbecue, including the cheese, brush it with butter or oil: this will greatly reduce the chances of its sticking. Put the pork loin on first. It should take about 3-4 minutes on one side, and 2-3 minutes on the other. Just before it is finished, cook the Halloumi. It should take 20-40 seconds per side. The pork loin and Halloumi are normally served together, with white retsina, red non-resinated wine, and pitta bread (warmed on the barbecue). Your guests should already have been into the dips described on page 48.

•

Next, put the pork kebabs on. They should take anything up to 10-15 minutes, being turned occasionally. Before you put them on, and while they are cooking, baste with oil/lemon mixture or the butter/garlic mixture or both, as you feel inclined. About 5 minutes after starting the pork, start the lamb cutlets: they should take 3-5 minutes on the first side, and 2-4 minutes on the second. Baste with oil/lemon mixture. If you are cooking steaks, give them 2-4 minutes on the first side, and 1-3 minutes on the second – or follow your (and your guests') preferences. Baste with the butter/garlic mixture. These meats can be served together as another course, with the accompaniments as before.

CARNITAS

Carnitas *or "little meats" are a favourite Mexican* antojito, *eaten with a cocktail stick (toothpick) or as a filling for a soft taco (see page 73). There are two ways of making them: the traditional way, which is best but tricky, and the way that most Mexicans actually make them.*

TRADITIONAL CARNITAS

1kg/2 lb boneless fatty pork (boned shoulder, etc.)
15ml.1 tbsp salt

Cut the meat into 2.5cm/1 in cubes. Put in a heavy pan with the salt, and just enough water to cover. Bring to the boil. Reduce the heat to a very slow simmer and stir occasionally until the water has evaporated. Continue to cook the *carnitas* over a low heat, so that the fat renders out – this is why you have to use a fatty cut. Eventually, you will be left with crispy yet tender nuggets of meat.

EASY CARNITAS

750g/1 1/2 lb good quality pork
1 small onion
5ml/1 tsp peppercorns
1 bay leaf
10ml/2 tsp salt
oil for deep-frying

Boil the meat with the onion, peppercorns, salt and bay leaf for about 1 hour. Use the smallest pot that will hold the meat, and use only enough water to cover the meat. It should be thoroughly cooked, but not actually falling apart. Leave it to cool in the cooking liquid.

•

When it is cool enough to handle, drain it carefully, pat it dry with paper towels, and with a very sharp knife, cut it into 2.5cm/1 in cubes. Deep-fry these in hot oil or lard for 45-90 seconds until well browned.

KALITSOUNIA

These are little turnovers or pasties of cottage cheese. The correct cheese to use is mitzithra, *which is a ewes' milk cheese with a pronounced flavour. We sometimes use home-made paneer, an Indian cheese, which closely approximates in texture if not in taste to* mitzithra. *There is something very satisfying about making everything from scratch.*

PANEER CHEESE

1.2 1/2 pts/5 cups extra rich (Jersey) milk   juice of 1 lemon
60ml/4 tbsp live (preferably Greek) yoghurt

DOUGH

200g/7 oz/2 cups plain (all-purpose) flour   5ml/1 tsp salt
30g/1 oz/ 2 tbsp butter   1 egg, beaten, for glazing
75ml/5 tbsp water   30g/1 oz sesame seeds for garnish

FILLING

250g/8 oz cottage cheese – or use the *paneer* above
salt and pepper to taste

First, make the cheese. If you cannot get extra-rich milk, mix some cream in with ordinary milk. Do not use homogenized milk or milk with additives in it. It is quite hard to make this cheese in the United States, because both the milk and the cream have been attenuated and "improved" almost beyond recognition in the name of "healthy" eating. For something even closer to *mitzithra*, use ewes' milk or goats' milk.

•

Heat the milk to boiling point; remove it from the heat, and stir it as it cools to keep a skin from forming. At blood heat, add the lemon juice and the yoghurt. Continue stirring until the cheese curdles.

•

Line a strainer with butter-muslin, and drain the cheese. When it is drained, squeeze gently in the cloth to remove further moisture. Leave it (in the cloth) under a heavy weight for at least 4 hours or overnight. The cheese is now ready for use.

•

Next, make the dough. Work the butter into the flour, then add the water. Knead the dough sparingly: do not overwork it. Roll out the dough to about 3mm/1/8 in thick, and with a small plate or large cutter, cut it into rounds approximately 10cm/4 in in diameter.

•

Mash the salt and pepper into the cheese, seasoning generously. Put a tablespoon of cheese in the middle of each round. Moisten the edges of the pastry with water, and fold over to make a D-shape. Pinch the edges together, or press them with a fork. Brush with beaten egg and sprinkle with sesame seeds. Bake in a preheated oven for 30 minutes at about 150°C/300°F/Mark 2.

VARIATION

Instead of brushing with egg and sprinkling with sesame seeds, you can fry the *kalitsounia* in a mixture of butter and olive oil. They would then traditionally be sprinkled with sugar before serving, which is better than it sounds but which you might care to try on just one piece before you sugar the lot.

BURRITOS AND CHIMICHANGAS

A burrito or "little donkey" is a large flour tortilla wrapped around the usual Mexican ingredients. A chimichanga is similar, only deep-fried – a sort of giant Mexican spring roll.

BURRITOS

4 large wheat tortillas, about 30cm/12 in in diameter (page 66)
500g/1 lb or 1 can refried beans (page 70)
150g/8 oz shredded meat (page 70)
100g/4 oz *guacamole* (page 51)
50-100g/2-4 oz cheese, grated
120ml/4 fl oz/1/2 cup soured (dairy sour) cream or *crema Mexicana*
ranchera sauce (see below) (optional)

The tortillas, beans and pork should be hot, and it is normal to heat the *burrito* through in the oven (or in the microwave) before serving.

•

Divide the beans and meat four ways. In the middle of each tortilla, make a small mound of beans about 15cm/6 in long and 5cm/2 in wide. Put the meat on top.

•

Fold the short "wings" either side of the ingredients inwards, then fold the longer "wings" one after the other to form the *burrito*. Serve with grated cheese and *guacamole* and soured (dairy sour) cream (or *creme Mexicana* or *crème fraîche* or similar) or better still with a ranchera sauce.

RANCHERA SAUCE

30ml/2 tbsp olive oil
200g/7 oz can tomatoes, drained and smashed
sugar if necessary
2-4 jalapeño or similar chillies, sliced
15ml/1 tbsp wine vinegar
salt and pepper to taste

Make this a day in advance, if possible, to allow the flavours to "marry". Fry the tomatoes in the olive oil until they form a thick paste. Add some sugar if the sauce is too sharp-tasting. Remove from the heat, add the chillies and vinegar, and mix well. Use hot or cold.

•

Ranchera sauce is also excellent for *Huevos rancheros*. Spread small corn tortillas (page 66) with refried beans (page 70) and put a fried egg on top of each. Dress with ranchera sauce. Serve two per person. *Machomo* (page 70) makes an excellent accompaniment.

CHIMICHANGAS

4 large wheat flour tortillas, about 30cm/12 in in diameter (page 66)
100-150g/4-6 oz cheese, grated
150-250g/6-8 oz refried beans (page 70)
120ml/4 fl oz/1/2 cup *crema Mexicana* or soured (dairy sour) cream
2 medium-sized tomatoes, finely chopped
100g/4 oz Chinese leaves (Nappa cabbage), shredded
175g/6 oz shredded meat (page 70) (optional)

1 small chilli pepper (optional)
1 avocado, chopped (optional)
15ml/1 tbsp plain (all-purpose) flour
about 15ml/1 tbsp of water
oil for deep-frying

Mix the flour and water to form a stiff paste for sealing the *chimichangas*.

•

Divide the remaining ingredients between the four tortillas. They should form a heap about 15ml/6 in long by 5cm/2 in wide by 4cm/1¹/₂ in deep. The usual order is a layer of beans; a layer of cheese; then a layer of lettuce, along with the tomato. The meat (if used) goes along the top of the lettuce: the pepper goes on top of that; and then the *crema Mexicana* and the chopped avocado (or *guacamole* – see page 51). Do not make the filling too uniform: part of the pleasure of a *chimichanga* is that each bite is different.

•

Form the *chimichanga* as for a *burrito*, but use the flour-and-water paste generously to secure the "wings". Deep-fry until golden brown. Drain well – they are inclined to be oily. Serve with beer or red wine.

PAKORAS

Pakoras are a great Indian appetizer, snack and light meal. They may be made from almost anything – chicken, cheese, or vegetables – coated in a gram flour batter and deep-fried, but the most popular pakoras *throughout the sub-continent are made with vegetables.*

PAKORA BATTER

5ml/1 tsp cumin seed (*jeera*)
5ml/1 tsp onion seed
5ml/1 tsp ground turmeric (*haldi*)
1 fresh chilli pepper, about 10cm/4 in long
1/3 cup gram flour (*besan*)
1/3 cup water
2.5ml/1/2 tsp salt
1.5ml/1/4 tsp garam masala

Roast the cumin, onion seed and turmeric powder together in a small iron pan for about 30 seconds. Remove the seeds from the chilli, and chop it finely. Mix the gram flour and water together: as long as the volumes are equal, the precise size of the cup does not matter. Add the spices, chopped chilli and salt. Mix thoroughly, then refrigerate for about 1 hour.

VEGETABLES

1/2 cauliflower
2 potatoes or sweet potatoes
4 baby or 1 small aubergine (eggplant)
4 small or 2 medium courgettes (zucchini)
1 medium onion
oil for frying

Break the cauliflower into florets. Peel the potatoes, and slice them diagonally. Slice the unpeeled aubergines (eggplants) lengthwise (for baby aubergines) or diagonally (for a large aubergine). Slice the courgettes (zucchini) diagonally. Peel the onion and slice it into rings.

•

Dip the vegetables into the batter, and fry them piece by piece in oil at 190ºC/375ºF. You can fry several pieces together, but always put each piece in individually or they will stick together.

•

Serve with hot chutneys – mango chutney is good. Beer goes very well with *pakoras*.

VARIATION

In India, we have had *pakoras* made from *paneer*, the cream cheese described on page 93: but we have never tried making them ourselves. An Indian friend assures us that the same batter works. You would need about half the quantities listed overleaf to make 100g/4 oz of cheese, enough for *pakoras*.

SAMOSAS

The best samosas we ever had were on a bus-trip between Dehra Dun and Delhi, and the second best are from our friend Mr Majorthi who has a shop in St Mark's Road in Easton, Bristol. One of the attractions of samosas, though, is that they never come out quite the same twice.

INGREDIENTS

2 small potatoes (about 250g/8 oz)
30ml/2 tbsp oil (mustard oil is good)
2.5ml/1/2 tsp black mustard seeds
1 medium onion, finely chopped
30-50g/1-2 oz ginger root
5ml/1 tsp fennel seed
1.5ml/1/4 tsp cumin seed
1.5ml/1/4 tsp ground turmeric

100g/4 oz fresh or thawed frozen green peas
15ml/1 tbsp finely chopped fresh coriander
2.5ml/1/2 tsp garam masala
pinch of hot red chilli powder
2.5ml/1/2 tsp salt, or to taste
15ml/1 tbsp water
8-12 spring roll skins
Flour-and-water paste (15ml/1 tbsp of each)

Boil the potatoes until they are tender but not fully cooked. Drain and cut into 1cm/1/2 in cubes.

•

Heat the oil in a heavy frying pan (skillet). When it is good and hot, add the mustard seeds. As soon as they begin to spit and burst, add the onion and the ginger. Stir constantly, and cook for 7-8 minutes until the mixture is soft and golden brown. Add the fennel, cumin and turmeric, then the potatoes, peas, salt and water. Cover tightly, and cook for 5 more minutes over a low heat. Add the coriander, and continue to cook until the peas are tender. Remove from the heat, and add the garam masala and red pepper. Allow to cool before using, or you will burn you fingers.

•

Roll a spring roll skin into a cone, and glue the edges with the flour-and-water paste. Fill it about three-quarters full, and fold the edges over; glue the final edge with the flour-and-water paste. Deep-fry in batches for 2-4 minutes until golden brown. Drain, and leave to cool for 1-2 minutes. Serve immediately, with chutneys, especially coriander chutney. They remain good for a few hours.

CORIANDER CHUTNEY

juice of 1 large or 2 small lemons
60ml/4 tbsp water
100g/4 oz fresh coriander (cilantro), coarsely chopped
60ml/4 tbsp finely chopped coconut or desiccated coconut
60ml/4 tbsp finely chopped onion
30g/1 oz ginger root, peeled and chopped
1-2 fresh hot chillies, finely chopped
5ml/1 tsp sugar
5ml/1 tsp salt
1.5ml/1/2 tsp freshly ground black pepper

Blend the lemon juice, water and coriander in a liquidizer or blender; add the coriander a bit at a time. When it is fully puréed, add the remaining ingredients and blend again. Add more sugar or salt to taste. This will keep for a week in the refrigerator.

SPANAKOKALITSOYNA

These Cretan spinach pies are made with a dough which contains much the same ingredients as filo, but which is not rolled out anything like as thinly. They are slightly more work then the spanakopittes on page 86, but it is the sort of cooking that makes you feel good.

PASTRY

250g/8 oz/2 cups plain (all-purpose) flour
30ml/2 tbsp olive oil
60ml/4 tbsp water
1 egg, beaten
flour for rolling the pastry

FILLING

750g/1 1/2 lb spinach
250g/8 oz cottage cheese
1 egg, beaten
30ml/2 tbsp olive oil
salt and pepper to taste
30g/1 oz sesame seeds for garnish

First, make the dough. Sift the flour and a pinch of salt into a large bowl. Rub the oil in with your fingers; the mixture should be quite grainy. Gradually mix in the water, and knead the dough on a floured pastry board or marble slab until it is smooth and elastic. If it is too sticky, add more flour. Cover and leave to rest for 30 minutes.

•

If it is fresh spinach, sprinkle it with salt, and rub the salt in with your hands. Leave it for 1 hour before squeezing it out. With thawed-out frozen spinach, just add salt to taste, but again squeeze well to remove excess water. Add the cottage cheese, egg, oil and seasoning. Mix well.

•

Roll out the dough on a floured board or marble slab, to about 3mm/1/8 in thick or less. Cut into 10-12cm/4-5 in squares; you should get about 12 squares. In the centre of each square, put a couple of tablespoons of the filling. Moisten the edges of the square with water, then fold the corners into the centre. Press the four flaps firmly together. Brush with egg, sprinkle with sesame seeds, and bake in a preheated oven at about 150ºC/300ºF/Mark 2 for 35 minutes. These are best served hot, but they are pretty good cold, too.

VARIATION

For a stronger flavour, substitute crumbled feta for part of the cottage cheese; anything from one-quarter to one-half of the total weight of cheese.

SPRING ROLLS

"Spring rolls" are traditionally served at spring festivals, but today these Chinese and Vietnamese delicacies appear at any time of year. They are surprisingly easy to make.

INGREDIENTS

20-25 spring roll skins
15ml/1 tbsp plain (all-purpose) flour
15ml/1 tbsp water
100g/4 oz pork or chicken
2-4 rashers bacon
250g/8 oz fresh or canned beansprouts
100g/4 oz peeled prawns
1 200g/7 oz can water chestnuts
6 spring onions (scallions)
30g/1 oz fresh ginger, finely chopped (optional)
15g/1/2 oz chopped coriander (optional)
oil (preferably sesame oil) for stir-frying
oil or lard for deep-frying
plum sauce, English mustard, chilli sauce as accompaniments

Frozen spring roll skins take about 30 minutes to defrost. Leftover skins can be re-frozen. Making your own can be difficult: it is hard to get them thin enough and tough enough.

•

Mix the flour and water together to make a thick paste or glue. This is used for sealing the spring rolls.

•

To make the filling, slice the meat and bacon into matchstick-sized pieces, and slice the water chestnuts as thinly as possible. Wash fresh beansprouts, or rinse canned ones; drain well. Chop the spring onions (scallions). Peel and finely chop the ginger. Stir-fry all the ingredients together. Put the meat and ginger in first, then add the other ingredients in turn, so that they are all cooked to the degree you like – it should not take more then 5-7 minutes overall.

•

Carefully peel off a spring roll skin; cover the remainder with a slightly damp tea towel (or cling film) to stop them drying out. Position the skin so that one corner is towards you. Put a large spoonful of cooked filling in this corner. Use a slotted spoon so that the mixture is not too wet. The precise quantity is a matter for experiment: if you overfill the rolls, they burst. Roll the corner towards the centre until the filling is just covered. Then fold the left and right corners inwards, and continue rolling the skin up. This is easier to do than describe: the secret is the diagonal rolling. Seal the flap (and repair any holes) with the flour-and-water paste.

•

In very hot oil (170-190°C/350-375°F), deep-fry the rolls until they are crispy and golden: typically 3-5 minutes. Do not overcook them, or the stuffing will begin to go dry, but do not undercook them or you will lose the contrast between crunchy skin and moist filling.

•

Serve immediately, accompanied with hot, spicy sauces for dipping: plum sauce and chilli sauce (available from oriental grocers), and English mustard mixed with water to a fairly soft consistency. Indian chutneys are also possibilities.

VARIATIONS

You can put just about what you like into a spring roll skin: mushrooms, bamboo shoots, green and red peppers, leftover meat, finely shredded *bok choy* (Chinese leaves, Nappa cabbage) or more – and you can vary the proportions wildly. We have even made cream cheese spring rolls. If you keep the skins in your freezer, you can make spring rolls from more or less whatever you have at hand.

•

Some people bind the filling with egg, and this is traditional in some areas, but there seems to be no advantage in it.

SPARE RIBS SZECHUAN

Much of the charm of Chinese spare ribs comes from repeated cooking, which is what makes the ribs tender and tasty. This version looks rather dry, but is actually very flavoursome, and much of the fat is removed. Most of the cooking can be done the day before and (as noted in the recipe) the braising sauce can be re-used several times.

RIBS

1.5kg/3 lb pork spare ribs, separated into individual ribs
oil for deep-frying, preferably groundnut (peanut oil)
spring onion for garnish

BRAISING SAUCE

1.75l/3 pts/4 US pints chicken stock
30ml/2 tbsp chilli bean sauce or 15 ml/1 tbsp chilli powder
20ml/4 tsp sugar
150ml/1/4 pt/2/3 cup dry sherry or rice wine
30ml/2 tbsp dark soy sauce
30ml/2 tbsp light soy sauce
4-6 cloves garlic, finely chopped
2-3 spring onions (scallions), finely chopped
30ml/2 tbsp whole yellow bean sauce
45ml/3 tbsp *hoisin* sauce

Deep-fry the spare ribs in batches: they should be brown and crisp. Drain well on kitchen paper.

•

Combine the chicken stock and the other ingredients, and bring to the boil in a large pan. Add the deep-fried spare ribs, cover, and simmer for up to 1 hour. Drain off the sauce; it can be frozen and re-used, and save a little to brush on the ribs for the final cooking, which can be done immediately or next day. This is very handy when you are expecting friends, but do not know when they will be arriving.

•

Grill (broil) or barbecue the ribs, or cook them in an oven preheated to 180°C/350°F/Mark 4, for 15 to 20 minutes before serving, basting with the braising sauce occasionally. Garnish with spring onions (scallions) and serve hot.

TEMPURA

Tempura – seafood and vegetables fried in a light, lacy batter – may seem quintessentially Japanese, but it is actually a Portuguese dish brought to Japan in the late sixteenth century. Even the name comes from the Quattuor Tempora, *the feast days of the Catholic Church when seafood was eaten.*

INGREDIENTS

350g/12 oz large raw prawn tails
1 large green pepper (bell pepper)
1 carrot
1 large courgette (zucchini)
250g/8 oz aubergine (eggplant)

1 medium-sized sweet potato
1 medium-sized onion
4 white or shiitake mushrooms
oil for frying

BATTER

2 egg yolks
450ml/3/4 pt/2 cups iced water

250g/8 oz/2 cups flour, sifted
75g/3 oz/3/4 cup flour for coating ingredients

DIPPING SAUCE

250ml/8 fl oz/1 cup *dashi*
15ml/1 tbsp *mirin* (cooking *sakê*)
30g/1 oz grated white radish (*daikon* or *mooli*)
10ml/2 tsp peeled, grated fresh ginger

45ml/3 tbsp light soy sauce
15ml/1 tbsp sugar

Make the dipping sauce first. Combine the liquid ingredients and the sugar; warm in a pan until the sugar is dissolved. Serve warm, with the *daikon* and the ginger on the side for the guests to add to their personal taste. You can buy *mirin* and "instant" *dashi* (just add hot water) in any shop that carries Japanese food.

•

Next, prepare the various ingredients to be fried. Score the prawns to stop them curling excessively when they are cooked. Or you can "butterfly" them by cutting them almost through lengthways and flattening them into wings. Core and de-seed the pepper; slice in strips from top to bottom. Scrape the carrot, and cut at an angle to create oval slices the thickness of a heavy coin. Slice the courgette (zucchini) the same way. If you are using the tiny Japanese aubergines (eggplants), slice them in halves or quarters. If you are using a single large aubergine (eggplant), peel it partially, leaving some skin on for decoration; halve it lengthways; and cut in slices 5mm/1/4 in thick. Depending on the size of the sweet potato, cut it either as for the carrot and courgette (zucchini), or as for the aubergine (eggplant). Slice the onion into rings. Halve the mushrooms if they are large.

•

Just before you are ready to cook, prepare the batter. Beat one of the egg yolks very lightly; add half the iced water; and finally beat in 100g/4 oz/1 cup of flour. Perhaps surprisingly, you do not mix the batter well: a batter that is too smooth will also be too dense. It is the little lumps of unmixed flour which give *tempura* batter its characteristic laciness. Make a second batch of batter only when the first is used up.

•

Heat the vegetable oil to 180°C/350°F. Use a light-flavoured oil such as groundnut (peanut); strong flavours will detract from the *tempura*. Dip the ingredients in flour, to help the batter stick, then in the batter. Fry them for about 3 minutes or until they are golden. Drain for a few seconds on kitchen paper, then serve immediately – *tempura* loses its charms pretty quickly. It is traditional to line the guests' plates with absorbent paper doilies, too.

VARIATIONS

You can cook almost anything *tempura*-style: squid, green beans, mange-tout peas (snow peas), ordinary potatoes, lotus root, other kinds of mushrooms, okra and small whole fish (whitebait or larger).

KALAMARES

Call them kalamares, lulas, *or what you will: tiny squid are an essential of most Mediterranean cuisines. They are fiddly to prepare, but home-fried kalamares are incomparably better than anything you will find outside a really good Greek taverna or Spanish tapas bar.*

INGREDIENTS

500g/1 lb small squid, up to about
    15cm/6 in long or 250g/8 oz
    ready-cleaned squid
Salt for cleaning the squid
    (about 50-100g/2-4 oz)
juice of 4 lemons

4 eggs
60ml/4 tbsp olive oil
5-10ml/1-2 tsp salt
pepper to taste
100g/14 oz/1 cup plain white flour
oil for deep-frying

Preparing the squid is time-consuming, but not difficult. It is much easier if you salt the squid liberally beforehand. Pull the tentacles and the body apart. Cut the tentacles at the base, leaving them all in one piece. Although the tentacles may lack aesthetic appeal, they are the best part of the squid and are avidly sought by connoisseurs.

•

Remove the "quill" and turn the body inside out to clean it thoroughly, Turn it right-side round again, and strip off the skin. Pull or cut off the fins. Rinse each squid in water after you have prepared it.

•

Put the squid bodies and tentacles in lemon juice. Leave them for anything from 15 minutes to several hours. The younger the squid, the less important it is to soak them, but older and tougher squid can profitably be soaked all day, or overnight.

•

Drain carefully, and pat dry with paper towels: wet squid will spit and splash when you fry them. Beat the eggs, the oil and the salt, together with pepper to taste. A teaspoon of salt is the minimum you will need to get a good flavour.

•

Cut the bodies into rings about 1cm/1/2 in thick: leave the tentacles in bunches. Dredge the squid in flour, then coat with egg. Heat the oil very hot, to 190ºC/375ºF, and fry the squid piece by piece. You can fry it in quite large batches, but it is important to put each piece into the oil individually, so they do not stick together.

•

The precise cooking time will depend on the tenderness of the squid and your own preferences: anything from 1 1/2 to 3 or 4 minutes. With young, tender squid, we favour the shorter time – it will be tenderer than you may have believed possible. Overcooking squid, on the other hand, will make it excessively chewy.

•

You can part-fry the squid in advance – anything from a few minutes to a whole day beforehand – and then re-fry them for a few seconds to reheat them and restore the crispness of the batter. Better still, you can re-fry much larger batches than you can handle for the initial frying, so it is quite easy to prepare enough squid for four people by frying them initially in two or three or even four batches, then re-frying the lot for thirty seconds just before you serve it.

•

This is quite a rich dish; serve it with something like stuffed tomatoes or a butterbean salad – and as part of a full-blown *mezedes*, page 91.

PÂTÉ OF SMOKED
AND FRESH SALMON

*This is a time-consuming and expensive dish to make, and very rich; but it is a treat for friends
who are seriously fond of their food. The recipe given below is enough for eight or even ten, or for
four to over-indulge. You cannot really make it any smaller, however.*

INGREDIENTS

15ml/1 tbsp olive oil
1 medium tomato
250g/8 oz fresh salmon, boneless and skinned
250g/8 oz smoked salmon (trimmings are fine)
1 large avocado
2 eggs
freshly ground white pepper
300ml/1/2 pt/1 1/4 cups double (heavy) cream
50g/2 oz cooked ham
butter
breadcrumbs

In a small frying pan (skillet), heat the oil. Skin and chop the tomato, and fry it
until it is soft – about 2-3 minutes. Force through a sieve: you need 60ml/4 tbsp of
tomato sauce for the recipe, and you can use the rest as a garnish.

•

Dice both lots of salmon, then blend in a food processor until smooth. Add the
eggs, tomato sauce and pepper. Blend thoroughly. Add the cream slowly, with the
processor running continuously. Dice the ham, add to the mixture, and blend in
coarsely.

•

Butter a medium-size loaf tin (pan) generously, and sprinkle the inside with
breadcrumbs. Choose a tin that is about three-quarters filled by the mixture –
about a 2l / 3 1/2 pt tin. Pour half the salmon mixture into it. Peel the avocado,
remove the stone and slice the flesh. Arrange the slices in an even layer over the
salmon mixture, then add the rest of the salmon. Cover the tin tightly with foil.

•

Cook in a *bain-marie* or steamer for 1 1/2–1 3/4 hours. Loosen the foil, and allow to
cool. Chill in the refrigerator: turn out of the mould and serve chilled and sliced.
This keeps for two or three days in the refrigerator.

CROQUETTES

Croquettes originated as a means of using up leftover cooked meat – especially the remains of the Sunday roast. Properly made, they are however a luxurious starter or light meal in their own right. You can use frozen leftover meat, or you can freeze the croquettes *after you make them.*

INGREDIENTS

300-400g/10-14 oz/2 cups cooked meat
1/2 small onion or 1 shallot
100g/4 oz/1/2 cup butter
6 rounded tablespoons plain
  (all-purpose) flour
250ml/8 fl oz/1 cup milk

2 eggs
100g/4 oz/2/3 cup fine breadcrumbs
2.5ml/1/2 tsp dried thyme or
  10ml/2 tsp fresh
2.5ml/1/2 tsp salt or to taste
oil for deep-frying

Dice the meat – lamb is our favourite, though beef and chicken are also good – then either put it through a mincer (grinder) or chop it very finely in the food processor. Chop the onion or shallot very finely indeed; keep it separate from the meat.

•

Make a *roux*, as follows. Melt the butter in a heavy saucepan over a gentle heat. Fry the onion or shallot in it, until it is so soft it has almost dissolved. Add the flour, and stir over a gentle heat until smooth. Stir in the milk to make a very thick white sauce: it should be so thick that it is sticky. For once, you do not have to worry about lumps – they will never show in the final croquettes.

•

Add the meat to the white sauce – there is no need to wait for it to cool – and continue cooking until the mixture is so thick that it starts to pull away from the sides of the pan. Leave to cool.

•

When it is cool enough to handle, wrap it in foil and chill it in the refrigerator for 1 hour or longer; you can leave it overnight if you want.

•

Beat the eggs with a teaspoon or so of water: this helps to keep the beaten eggs thin enough to use easily. Form the meat-roux mixture into sausage-shaped croquettes 8-10cm/3-4 in and about 3cm/1 1/4 in in diameter. You should end up with 8 croquettes, though you can make them smaller if you wish. Dip them in beaten egg, then roll them in breadcrumbs. For an extra-crunchy covering, repeat: roll them in egg a second time, then in breadcrumbs again.

•

Let them stand for at least 15 minutes (they can be frozen at this stage), then deep-fry in oil at about 190°C/375°F. Serve hot, with a warning that you can burn your mouth on them if you eat them too soon. Garnish with salad and serve with tomato ketchup or a home-made tomato sauce; both the sauce for *bragoli* (page 87) and the Mexican cooked *salsa* (page 51) are particularly good with beef.

VARIATIONS

You can vary the spicing to suit the meat. With lamb, try thyme, rosemary or cumin. With beef, try adding a couple of cloves of finely chopped garlic fried with the onion or shallot. For chicken, try parsley or sage or both – or chopped fresh coriander (cilantro) if (as we are) you are a coriander addict.

CHAWAN MUSHI

Chawan mushi is a sort of Japanese egg custard, flavoured with fish stock and containing chicken, prawns and other ingredients. It can be cooked quite firm, or it can be almost a soup, barely set at all. It is easier to make than it sounds. Dashi *is a stock made from dried bonito and a kind of seaweed. You can buy sachets of ready-made* dashi *concentrate in most Japanese stores.*

INGREDIENTS

3 eggs
600ml/ 1 pt/2 1/2 cups *dashi*
20ml/4 tsp Japanese soy sauce
100g/4 oz chicken meat (leg or breast)
15ml/1 tsp *mirin* (cooking *saké*)

4 prawn tails, each about 5cm/2 in long
4 button mushrooms
4 gingko nuts (optional)
1 spring onion (scallion)

Beat the eggs thoroughly, then stir in the *dashi* and the soy sauce. Strain the mixture: a tea strainer is ideal.

•

Slice the chicken into matchsticks or small cubes, and leave it to marinade for a few minutes in the *saké*. In small bowls or cups, place one peeled prawn tail; one quarter of the diced chicken; one button mushroom; and one gingko nut if you can get them (they are more important for authenticity than for anything else – it still tastes good without them). Pour the strained egg/*dashi* mixture over, so that the cups are about four-fifths full. Chop the spring onion (scallion) into small rings, and scatter over the top. In Japan, there are special lidded *chawan mushi* bowls, but if you cannot get bowls with lids, then make lids out of aluminium foil.

•

Heat water in a steamer. When it is boiling, put the *chawan mushi* bowls in. Steam for about 10 minutes. the *chawan mushi* is cooked when, if you prick the custard with a thin skewer, clear juice runs out. Once you have established the correct cooking time for your steamer and bowls, you will not need to worry about testing to see if it is cooked. You normally eat it with a spoon and chopsticks.

VARIATIONS

You can put various things into *chawan mushi*, such as smaller shrimps or prawns, ham, pork, fish and so forth. You can also garnish it in different ways. After it is cooked, you can put slices of lemon peel or fresh ginger root on top, cut into broad, flat matchsticks.

SATAY

Satay is a Malaysian dish, consisting of small bamboo skewers of marinated meat or chicken, or whole prawns, served with a peanut sauce. It is one of those things which is almost never served in large enough quantities in restaurants! You are unlikely to want to make all the varieties listed below, at least simultaneously. Two is often enough: beef and chicken, say, or pork and prawn.

MEAT

350g/12 oz high-quality boneless beef	350g/12 oz boneless chicken
350g/12 oz high-quality boneless pork	(breasts are ideal)
350g/12 oz high-quality boneless lamb	250g/8 oz shelled raw prawn tails (about 12)

Cut the meat or chicken into small dice, about 1cm/1/2 in on a side. Use the prawns whole. Soak bamboo skewers in water for at least half an hour (this will stop them burning too fast) and thread the meat on to the skewers: one kind of meat per skewer. Marinate (see below) for at least 1 hour, turning occasionally. Finally, barbecue or grill (broil) briefly until just cooked, and serve with the peanut sauce, below.

BEEF MARINADE

2.5ml/1/2 tsp tamarind extract	5ml/1 tbsp sugar
30ml/2 tbsp hot water	3 cloves garlic
juice of 1/2 lemon	1 onion, chopped
60ml/4 tbsp soy sauce	salt and pepper to taste

Dilute the tamarind extract in the hot water. Mix all the ingredients together in a blender or liquidizer.

PORK MARINADE

60ml/4 tbsp oil (preferably sesame oil)	5ml/1 tsp aniseed
60ml/4 tbsp soy sauce	2 cloves garlic
45ml/3 tbsp honey	salt and pepper to taste
30ml/2 tbsp vinegar	ginger root

Blend all the ingredients together in a liquidizer or blender. Squeeze a small piece of very fresh ginger root in a garlic press and add the juice to the mixture.

LAMB MARINADE

1 onion, chopped
60ml/4 tbsp groundnut (peanut) oil

60ml/4 tbsp soy sauce
salt and pepper to taste

Blend all the ingredients in a liquidizer or blender.

CHICKEN MARINADE

60ml/4 tbsp soy sauce
15ml/1 tbsp honey
30ml/2 tbsp ginger juice (use a garlic press)

30ml/2 tbsp rice wine or dry sherry
chilli powder or black pepper
salt to taste

Blend all the ingredients in a liquidizer or blender.

PRAWN MARINADE

75ml/5 tbsp soy sauce
15ml/1 tbsp ginger juice (use a garlic press)
45ml/3 tbsp rice wine or dry sherry
2 cloves garlic, (optional)
2 fresh green chillies, (optional)
salt and pepper to taste

Chop the garlic and chillies, if using, then blend all the ingredients in a liquidizer or blender.

PEANUT SAUCE

Part 1

2 medium-sized onions
4-6 cloves garlic (or more!)
4 fresh hot red chillies (or more!)
15ml/1 tbsp (or more!) shrimp paste (from oriental shops)
10ml/2 tsp ground coriander
10ml/2 tsp ground cumin
5ml/1 tsp dried fennel
60ml/4 tbsp oil for frying

Part 2

175g/6 oz creamed coconut
250ml/8 fl oz/1 cup hot water
10ml/2 tsp tamarind extract
30ml/2 tbsp ginger juice (use a garlic press)
30ml/2 tbsp (or more!) sugar
350g/12 oz of crunchy peanut butter
juice of 1 lime
grated zest of 1 lemon
salt and pepper to taste

All the ingredients marked (or more!) would probably be increased significantly for Malaysian tastes, but represent a good starting point. Making the peanut sauce is the most time-consuming and difficult part of the recipe, and you may prefer to use bottled peanut sauce. It is not quite as good as home-made, but if you do not have the time to make it yourself, it is still better than no sauce.

•

Break up the creamed coconut with a knife, and dissolve it in the hot water (use a microwave). Dissolve the tamarind extract in 45-60ml/3-4 tbsp of hot water.

•

Purée together all the ingredients for Part 1, except the oil, in a food processor or blender. Fry the resulting paste in the oil until it is strongly aromatic. Add all the ingredients from Part 2. Simmer together for 10 minutes: add enough water to make the mixture thin enough to stir easily. The sauce should be thick and grainy, like a Dijon mustard.

IDLI

Idli (steamed dumplings made from fermented rice batter) are one of the staples of South Indian tiffin. They are easy to make, but involve many hours of waiting time – you really need to start two days in advance. The easiest way to cook them, if you do not have an idli *pan, is to use an egg poacher.*

INGREDIENTS

275g/9 oz/1 1/3 cups basmati rice
175g/6 oz/1 cup *urid dal* (split black gram)
5ml/1 tsp fenugreek seeds
2.5ml/1/2 tsp bicarbonate of soda (baking soda)
salt to taste
15ml/1 tbsp melted butter

Pick over and wash the rice and the dal (both are obtainable in Indian shops). Soak the rice, dal and fenugreek seeks for at least 6 hours, and preferably overnight. Drain well, but keep the water. Grind the rice, dal, fenugreek seeds, bicarbonate of soda and salt together in a food processor, adding some of the soaking water as necessary to make a smooth paste. You can now throw away any remaining soaking water. Put the paste in a very large bowl, covered with a damp cloth, and leave it overnight. It will ferment and expand considerably.

•

Next day, mix the batter well. The consistency should be that of thick pouring cream. Thin further with water if necessary.

•

Lightly butter the inside of the egg-poaching cups, and fill them three-quarters full with batter. Steam for 10-15 minutes, and serve with *sambhar* (see below) or any vegetable curry.

SAMBHAR

250g/8 oz/1 1/3 cups red lentils
8 okra
250g/8 oz white radish (*mooli*)
1 onion
4 tomatoes
1 bell pepper
10ml/2 tsp sambhar masala (opposite)
2.5ml/1/2 ground turmeric
500ml/17 fl oz/2 1/4 cups water
250g/8 oz cauliflower florets
30ml/2 tbsp tamarind juice
5ml/1 tsp brown sugar

*60ml/4 tbsp vegetable oil
*2.5ml/1/2 tsp mustard seeds
*2 small, dried red chillies
*2.5ml/1/2 tsp cumin seed
*6 curry leaves
*2 cloves garlic, crushed or finely sliced
*pinch of asafoetida (*heeng*)
salt
crisp-fried onions and coriander leaves for garnish

Pick over and wash the lentils. Top and tail the okra. Peel the white radish and slice into 2.5cm/1 in pieces. Peel the onion and slice it thickly. Quarter the tomatoes. Core and de-seed the pepper, and cut it into large pieces. You can substitute or add other vegetables, such as aubergines (eggplants), potatoes, courgettes (zucchini), or whatever you like.

•

Put the lentils, sambhar masala, turmeric and water in a pan, and bring to the boil. Simmer for about 20-25 minutes until the lentils are mushy and a good deal of the water has evaporated. Mash the lentils in the fluid – a food processor makes this easy. You can freeze some or all of the lentils at this stage to save time another day. We typically cook 1kg/2 1/4 lb at a time.

•

Add the okra, cauliflower, white radish, onion, tamarind juice and sugar, and salt to taste; it takes quite a lot of salt. If you are using tamarind concentrate, dilute 2.5ml/1/2 tsp in boiling water to make 30ml/2 tbsp. Cook for another 10-15 minutes until the vegetables are done, then add the tomatoes and pepper.

•

In a small frying pan (skillet), heat all the asterisked ingredients together until the mustard seeds begin to pop and the chillies start to darken. Pour this over the curry (stand back – it spits) and cover immediately to allow the aroma to suffuse into the dish. Garnish with onions, fried until they are brown and crisp, and fried coriander leaves.

SAMBHAR MASALA

90ml/6 tbsp coriander seeds
20 black peppercorns
2.5ml/1/2 asafoetida (*heeng*)
8 curry leaves
7.5ml/1 1/2 tsp fenugreek seeds (*methi*)
10ml/2 tsp white cumin seeds
10ml/2 tsp ground turmeric
10ml/2 tsp mustard seeds
15-30ml/1-2 tbsp torn-up hot red chillies
15ml/1 tbsp each dried black beans, lentils and chickpeas (garbanzo beans)

In a heavy iron pan, "dry-fry" each ingredient separately until it begins to brown and give off a characteristic aroma. Grind them all together in an electric coffee grinder or with a mortar and pestle. Store in an airtight jar.

BLINI

*Blini – buckwheat pancakes served with a variety of toppings – are a feast, rather than a meal.
You need to eat them in the kitchen, with the cook turning them out and people adding their own
toppings as they go; it is a great way to run an informal party. There is a lot of preparation and
waiting time, but you can do most of the work the previous day. And they are delicious!*

BATTER

30g/1 oz/2 tbsp butter
300g/10 oz/2 1/2 cups plain (all-purpose) flour
1l/13/4 pts/just over 2 US pints milk
6g/1/4 oz dried yeast (one packet)
2.5ml/1/2 tsp salt
100g/4 oz/1 cup buckwheat flour
2 eggs, separated
1.5ml/1/4 tsp sugar
butter for greasing pan

TOPPINGS

caviar
smoked salmon (trimmings are fine)
smoked trout
other smoked fish
taramasalata
crème fraîche or soured (dairy sour) cream
melted butter

Melt the butter in a small saucepan. Add 300ml/1/2 pt/1 1/4 cups milk, and warm
to blood heat. Add the milk to 200g/7 oz/2 cups of the plain flour. In a deep
mixing bowl. Beat well to avoid lumps.

•

Sprinkle on the yeast and add half the salt. Mix well. Put the bowl in a warm place,
under a cover, until the dough has doubled in bulk: this should take about 1 hour.

•

Warm another 300ml/1/2 pt/1 1/4 cups of milk in a small saucepan. Work the rest
of the flour into the dough, along with the buckwheat flour, the egg yolks and the
warm milk. Add the flour and the milk gradually and alternately, to avoid lumps. If
you need it, add a little more warm milk to make a thick pancake batter. Add the
rest of the salt, and the sugar. Leave to rise for a further 2 hours, or overnight.

•

An hour before you want to cook the blini, warm 150ml/1/4 pt/2/3 cup of milk to
just below boiling point, and whisk it into the batter. Also whisk the egg-whites until
stiff, and fold them gently into the batter. Do not beat the batter again! Let it rest
for 10 minutes; it will keep overnight in the refrigerator, but no longer.

•

Lightly grease a heavy pan or griddle with butter, and drop the batter on to it to
make the blini. Use only about 15ml/1 tbsp of batter at a time: blinis swell as they
cook. Cook for 2-3 minutes per side. Serve immediately. You can keep them warm
in a preheated oven at 160°C/325°F/Mark 3, but the texture will not be as good as
if they were served hot from the pan – and if you have gone to this much trouble
already, why compromise?

Chapter Five

SAUCES, DRESSINGS AND PICKLES

Vinaigrette

VINAIGRETTE

Vinaigrette and mayonnaise are the two basic dressings. A good vinaigrette is a revelation, but a bad vinaigrette – corn oil and harsh vinegar – can be disgusting. The best vinaigrettes are as easy to make as the worst; they just call for better ingredients.

INGREDIENTS

oil (olive, walnut, sunflower ...)
wine vinegar (balsamic, sherry, flavoured ...)
salt

pepper (optional)
mustard powder (optional)

Dissolve the salt in a little vinegar, and mix three parts of oil with one part vinegar. The proportions may be varied. The minimum you generally need to dress a salad are 90ml/6 tbsp of oil and 30ml/2 tbsp vinegar.

•

Grind a little pepper into the mixture from a pepper mill. Mix thoroughly. A little dry mustard powder, perhaps 1.5ml/1/4 tsp to 120ml/4 fl oz/1/2 cup of dressing, will flavour the vinaigrette (surprisingly slightly) and delay its re-separation into its component parts (surprisingly efficiently). Never keep vinaigrettes more than a day or two; the flavour deteriorates.

VARIATIONS

There are probably more variations of vinaigrette sauce than there are cooks, because no two people use exactly the same proportions of vinegar and oil, and most cooks are not even particularly consistent from one time to the next. Also, you can use a wide variety of different oils, and at least as wide a variety of vinegars; and you can add different flavourings, as you feel inclined.

•

You do not even have to use oil and vinegar: lemon or lime juice, or verjus (the juice of unripe grapes) or cheap red wine can replace the vinegar, and cream can replace the oil. If you are using lemon juice, verjus, etc., then the proportion is half and half oil and juice. To make a cream vinaigrette mix four parts cream to one part vinegar.
A mustard and cream vinaigrette is made with 15ml/1 tbsp of French mustard, 45ml/3 tbsp of cream and up to 15ml/1 tbsp of wine vinegar, seasoned with salt and pepper. Some people add brandy to a vinaigrette.

•

Other possibilities include: garlic, finely sliced or crushed: or finely chopped shallots; or capers or cornichons, again finely chopped; or mashed anchovies; or mashed hard-boiled egg; or herbs such as chives, chervil, parsley, mint, tarragon, oregano and thyme. For a curry flavour, take 15ml/1 tbsp of finely chopped onion, and fry it until it is soft in 15ml/1 tbsp of oil mixed with 5ml/1 tsp of curry powder, taking care not to burn the curry powder. Mix this with the vinaigrette.

SOME VINAIGRETTE DISHES

Any vinaigrette may be used to dress almost any salad, but a cream vinaigrette is especially good with cos (romaine) lettuce, and a mustard and cream vinaigrette goes well with baby beetroot (red beets), celeriac, chicory (endive) or potato. Freshly cooked vegetables (carrots, potatoes, beans, asparagus, peas, or baby beetroot (red beets) – all cooked *separately*) can be mixed and dressed with a vinaigrette. A useful trick is to add chopped or grated nuts to any salad before dressing with vinaigrette.

Plain boiled leeks, served warm or cold (not hot) with a garlic vinaigrette, are unexpectedly good. Use a strong-tasting vinegar – cider is ideal – and a good olive oil. Leeks vinaigrette taste light in summer and hearty in winter, which is a useful accomplishment.

•

Asparagus, again served warm or cold, is very good with a mild vinaigrette made from walnut oil and sherry vinegar.

•

Brawn or head cheese is much improved with a sharp vinaigrette, preferably made with lemon juice or verjus and the minimum of oil; garnish generously with capers and cornichons. Cold tongue benefits from a milder vinaigrette, made perhaps with olive oil and sherry vinegar.

MAYONNAISE

The best mayonnaise is made only with egg yolks and first-quality olive oil.
Flavour mayonnaise with garlic to make aïoli.

BASIC MAYONNAISE

2 egg yolks
30ml/2 tbsp good-quality white wine vinegar

1.5ml/1/4 tsp dry mustard (optional)
300ml/1/2 pt/1 1/4 cups mild olive oil

Beat the egg yolks, add the vinegar and beat until well mixed. Beat in the mustard.

•

Very slowly, beating constantly, add the olive oil. You can use extra virgin oil, but the flavour will be too strong for most people, and the colour will be greenish-yellow. One function of the vinegar is to lighten the colour.

•

Although there is a lot of mystique about making mayonnaise, it really is not difficult. There are two things to remember. The first is that it is almost impossible to add the oil too slowly. To begin with, add a teaspoon or so at a time in a slow drizzle; later, you can speed up the addition of oil. The second thing is not to lose your nerve: keep pouring the oil in, and the mayonnaise *will* thicken.

•

If you get it wrong, and the mayonnaise curdles, no amount of beating will restore it, Just beat another egg, though, and add the curdled mayonnaise slowly to that, beating as before. It will un-curdle and become smooth, but you will end up with a great deal of mayonnaise.

AÏOLI

1-2 cloves garlic
2 egg yolks
30ml/2 tbsp good-quality white wine vinegar

300ml/1/2 pt/1 1/4 cups olive oil
1.5ml/1/4 tsp dry mustard (optional)

Crush, pound or liquidize the garlic, then follow exactly the same method as for mayonnaise. This makes an excellent dip, and is one of those occasion when a really thick, rich extra virgin oil is a good idea; so is tarragon vinegar.

IMPROVING COMMERCIAL MAYONNAISE

120ml/4 fl oz/1/2 cup good-quality commercial mayonnaise
30ml/2 tbsp olive oil

Most good-quality commercial mayonnaises (not salad creams) can be improved by beating in 10 to 20 per cent (by volume) of extra virgin olive oil. The advantage of this is that it is quick and easy and makes a modest quantity of very acceptable mayonnaise – some people prefer it to the home-made variety.

EGGS MAYONNAISE

4, 6 or 8 eggs
120-150ml/4-5 fl oz/1/2–2/3 cup mayonnaise (page 115)
50g/2 oz jar lumpfish caviar (optional)

Hard-boil the eggs, allow them to cool, then peel and halve them. Arrange two, three or four halves on each person's plate, and pour one-quarter of the mayonnaise over each plate full. For a luxurious garnish, divide the contents of the jar of lumpfish roe evenly between the plates. Do not make this dish too far in advance, and do not add the caviar until the last minute or the colour may run. We prefer this dish at room temperature, rather than chilled.

•

Alternative garnishes include a quarter of a teaspoonful of finely chopped anchovies, or a tablespoon (or more) of slivered smoked salmon. Or serve with smoked fish as a rich, filling meal.

KIMCHI

Kimchi – Korean pickled cabbage – is eaten as a dish in its own right, as well as being an accompaniment to almost everything Koreans eat. A bowl of kimchi *is easy to eat, low in calories, and leaves you with the distinct impression that you have had a full meal. The quantities given below will fill two 1 litre/1 3/4 pint jars.*

INGREDIENTS

1 large head Chinese leaves (Nappa cabbage)
1 large white radish (*daikon* or *mooli*)
2 fresh red or green chillies (red is prettier)
2 thumb-sized pieces of fresh ginger root
30ml/2 tbsp red chilli powder

1 cucumber
50g/2 oz salt
2 cloves garlic

Wash the Chinese leaves (Nappa cabbage) and shred them in strips 3–5mm/1/8–1/4 in wide. Peel the white radish, quarter it lengthways, and chop it into sections up to 1cm/1/2 in thick. Quarter the cucumber lengthways and chop as for the radish. Place in a large vessel with the salt. Toss well, so that everything is evenly coated with salt, and leave for up to 2 hours. It will "weep" copiously.

•

Drain and squeeze lightly to get rid of excess salt. Remove the seeds from the red or green chillies, and chop them finely. Peel the garlic and ginger, and slice very thinly or chop finely. Mix the chopped chilli, chilli powder, garlic and ginger with the salted vegetables.

•

Pack into jars and leave at room temperature for one or two days (three days in a cool room), loosely capped. The cabbage will start to ferment, which smells awful and builds up quite a pressure. Once it is well under way, you can screw the lid down tighter and refrigerate the *kimchi*. It will be ready to eat after two or three days, but will continue to improve for a week or more and will keep for several weeks.

If your *kimchi* is too hot, reduce the spices next time – but you will find that you soon build up a positively Korean tolerance for the stuff. Yoghurt is good for cooling your mouth while you are learning.

PICKLED OKRA

Okra, or ladies' fingers, are pickled in the American south and south-west. They make an excellent addition to the usual bowls of peanuts, olives etc. that you can set out at a moment's notice while preparing something else at ten minutes' notice. The quantities given below will fill three 500ml/16 fl oz preserving jars, though you might as well make half a dozen jars while you are at it.

INGREDIENTS

750g/1 1/2 lb okra
few sprigs of fresh dill (optional)
2 or more dried red chilli peppers (optional)
5ml/1 tsp mustard seed
1-3 cloves garlic

pinch of alum
450ml/3/4 pt/ 2 cups cider vinegar
250ml/8 fl oz/1 cup water
30-45ml/2-3 tbsp salt

Wash the okra and trim off the very ends of the stems. Pack them point-down in the preserving jars, tightly but without crushing them, together with a sprig or two of dill leaves or dill flowers, if using.

•

Tear up the chillies. Remove the seeds if you want a milder pickle, or omit the chillies altogether for a very mild taste. Slice the garlic. Boil all the ingredients except the okra together. When they come to the boil, pour the liquid over the okra, covering it completely. Cap tightly, and store the jars upside-down for at least two weeks. The pickled okra will continue to improve for many weeks, and will keep for months – or as long as you can resist opening them. Serve chilled: they will be crisper that way. In any case, refrigerate after opening.

FETA IN OIL

Feta cubes preserved in oil are available commercially, but you can make them better (and cheaper) yourself, using extra virgin olive oil and your own preferred seasoning. You can serve them in their own right like olives, or use them in salads or to garnish all kinds of other dishes.

INGREDIENTS

100g/4 oz feta cheese
1 fresh or dried red chilli pepper
1-3 cloves garlic
250ml/8 fl oz/1 cup olive oil
15-30ml/1-2 tbsp chopped fresh thyme

Cut the cheese into 1-2cm/1/2–3/4 in cubes. Chop the chilli pepper, removing the seeds if you do not want a hot oil. Slice the garlic thinly.

•

Pour the oil into a jar, and add the cheese and other ingredients, taking care that they are well mixed. You can, of course, use other herbs to suit yourself: try oregano, rosemary, and dill, for example, Do not pack the cheese too tightly, or it will stick together. Make sure the oil covers the cheese completely; this is important for preservation.

•

Leave at room temperature for at least 24 hours; this will keep for days or even weeks without refrigeration. If you do refrigerate it, it will keep for months but you must allow it to come to room temperature before you try to use it, or the oil will be glutinous and unattractive. When the cheese is finished, the oil makes an impressive salad dressing.

Appendix

AMERICAN DISHES
Chicken and Avocado Salad 31
Fried Potato Skins 79
Pickled Okra 117
Sausage and Beans 74

BRITISH DISHES
Anchovy and Cream Savoury 37
Scotch Eggs 77
Welsh Rarebit 35

CHINESE DISHES
Brocolli and Sesame 36
Spare Ribs Szechuan 101
Spring Rolls 100

EAST EUROPEAN DISHES
Aubergine "Caviar" 27
Beetroot and Walnut Salad 32
Blini with Caviar 112
Fish *Zakuski* with Dill Sauce 23
Lumpfish "Caviar" 14
Potato and Egg Salad 52
Potato and Beetroot Salad 52
Potato and Tuna Salad 52
True Sturgeon Caviar 14

FRENCH DISHES
Artichokes 34
Croquettes 106
Crudités with Cold Anchovy Sauce 26
Deep-fried Camembert 34
Eggs *en Cocotte* 54
Feuilleté of Scrambled Egg and Smoked
    Fish 15
French Bean Salad 38
Hot Bean and Almond Salad 38
Mayonnaise 115
Palm Heart and Artichoke Salad 21
Ratatouille 65
Rosbif Mayonnaise 41
Scallops in Cheese and Sherry Sauce 63
Vinaigrette 114

GREEK AND MIDDLE EASTERN DISHES
Barbecued *Mezé* 91
Dolmades 89

Eggs with Courgettes 58
Eggs with Tomatoes 58
Falafel 75
Feta in Oil 118
Hummus 48
Kalamares 104
Kalitsounia 93
Mushrooms à la Grècque 28
Olives in Spiced Vinegar 16
Olives with Thyme 17
Spanakokalitsoyna 99
Spanokopittes 86
Taramasalata 48
Tzatziki 49

INDIAN DISHES
Idli 110
Pakoras 96
Samosas with Coriander Chutney 98
Seekh Kebab 78

ITALIAN DISHES
Antipasto Misto 18
Bagna Cauda 24
Basic Pasta Salad 47
Bragoli 87
Bruschetta 20
Carpaccio 28
Carpaccio in Mayonnaise 29
Chicken Pasta Salad 47
Cooked Fennel and Dolcelatte 40
Crostini 62
Fennel, Cheese and Green Olives 40
Fried Mozzarella 35
Grissini 59
Marinated *Carpaccio* 29
Mixed *Spiedini* 60
Mozzarella and Aubergine 19
Mozzarella and Bread 19
Mozzarella con Melone 19
Proscuitto *con Melone* 16
Prawn *Spiedini* 60
Stuffed *Bragoli* and tomato sauce 87

JAPANESE DISHES
Chawan Mushi 107
Sashimi 84
Sushi 84
Tempura 102

KOREAN DISH
Kimchi 116

MALAY DISH
Satay with Peanut Sauce 108

MEXICAN DISHES
Basic *Quesadillas* 68
Burritos 94
Carne Molida Cruda 67
Carnitas 92
Chimichangas 94
Chiles Rellenos 88
Cooked Tomato Salsa 51
Corn Tortillas 66
Frijoles Fritos 70
Guacamole 51
Nachos 70, 71
Quesadillas de Luxe 68
Quesadillas Sincronizadas 68
Salsa Fresca 51
Shredded meat and *machomo* 70, 71
Tacos 73
Tostadas 73
Tostaditas 73
Wheat Flour Tortillas 66

SCANDANAVIAN DISHES
Basic Rollmops 22
Smoked Herring 15
Smoked Salmon 14
Smoked Trout 15

SPANISH DISHES
Albondiguitas 76
Garlic Shrimp with Butter 82
Garlic Shrimp with olive oil 82
Hot Peppers Stuffed with Cream Cheese 80
Mushrooms Stuffed with Sausage 55
Roasted Pepper Salad 45

OTHER DISHES
Braised Fennel 44
Butter Bean Salad 38
Canned Bean Salad 39
Fennel, Rice and Egg Salad 40
Paté of Smoked and Fresh Salmon 105
Prawn Cocktail 56
Stuffed Tomatoes with Cottage Cheese 42
Stuffed Tomatoes with Egg and Mayonnaise 42
Stuffed Tomatoes with Tuna and Beetroot 42
Stuffed Tomatoes with Tuna and Mayonnaise 42

Blini with caviar